W9-CAJ-427

Grandma Jo's

Soup Kettle

ALSO BY JOANNA M. LUND

The Healthy Exchanges Cookbook
HELP: The Healthy Exchanges Lifetime Plan
Cooking Healthy with a Man in Mind
Cooking Healthy with the Kids in Mind
Dessert Every Night!
The Diabetic's Healthy Exchanges Cookbook
The Strong Bones Healthy Exchanges Cookbook
The Arthritis Healthy Exchanges Cookbook
The Heart Smart Healthy Exchanges Cookbook
The Best of Healthy Exchanges Food Newsletter '92 Cookbook
Letters from the Heart
It's Not a Diet, It's a Way of Life (audiotape)

Alan Ehrenhalt is executive editor of *Governing* magazine in Washington, D.C. Born in 1947 in Chicago, he received his bachelor's degree from Brandeis University and his master's degree from the Columbia University School of Journalism. He has been a reporter for the Associated Press, *Congressional Quarterly,* and the *Washington Star,* and for twelve years was political editor of *Congressional Quarterly.* He has also been a Nieman Fellow at Harvard University and a visiting scholar at the University of California, Berkeley. Ehrenhalt's first book, *The United States of Ambition,* was a finalist for the 1991 *Los Angeles Times* Book Prize and was a *New York Times* Notable Book of the Year. He lives in Arlington, Virginia, with his wife and two daughters.

Grandma Jo's

Soup Kettle

100 Hearty and

Healthy Soups,

Stews, Gumbos,

and Chowders

A HEALTHY EXCHANGES® COOKBOOK

JoAnna M. Lund

HELPing Others HELP Themselves
the **Healthy Exchanges**® Way™

A Perigee Book

A Perigee Book
Published by The Berkley Publishing Group
A member of Penguin Putnam Inc.
375 Hudson Street
New York, New York 10014

Copyright © 1999 by Healthy Exchanges, Inc.
Diabetic Exchanges calculated by Rose Hoenig, R.D., L.D.
Cover design by Charles Björklund
Cover art by Charles Björklund and Joe Krantz
Front-cover author photograph by Glamour Shots® of West Des Moines

All rights reserved. This book, or parts thereof,
may not be reproduced in any form without permission.

For more information about Healthy Exchanges products, contact:
Healthy Exchanges, Inc.
P.O. Box 124
DeWitt, Iowa 52742-0124
(319) 659-8234

Perigee Special Sales edition: January 1999
ISBN: 0-399-52525-4
Published simultaneously in Canada.

The Penguin Putnam Inc. World Wide Web site address is
http://www.penguinputnam.com

Printed in the United States of America

10 9 8 7 6 5 4 3 2 1

Before using the recipes and advice in this book, consult your physician or health-care provider to be sure they are appropriate for you. The information in this book is not intended to take the place of any medical advice. It reflects the author's experiences, studies, research, and opinions regarding a healthy lifestyle. All material included in this publication is believed to be accurate. The publisher assumes no responsibility for any health, welfare, or subsequent damage that might be incurred from the use of these materials.

This cookbook is dedicated to the entire QVC "family," from the viewers who love my easy "common folk" healthy recipes, to the book buyers who are always interested in my newest projects, to the show hosts who are so delightful to work with, to the production staff who work so hard to ensure everything goes as planned without a glitch, and to the hardworking order representatives answering the phones. Each of you is a vital part of our recipe for success.

Contents

Acknowledgments

I'm so thankful to all the wonderful people at QVC who help me share my "common folk" healthy recipe books with you—throughout the year *and* on those oh-so-special days that I get to offer you my Today's Special Value trio of books. For helping me get my collection of cookbooks ready for that glorious moment the floor producer says, "You're on," I want to thank:

Paula Piercy and Karen Foner from QVC, for giving my books the honor of being a TSV, and John Duff and Barbara O'Shea from Putnam, for helping me get those books published quickly so they are ready for the big day.

Angela Miller and Coleen O'Shea, for believing in this middle-aged grandma from Iowa who writes in a "Grandma Moses" style.

Rita Ahlers, Connie Schultz, Shirley Morrow, Lori Hansen, and all my other Healthy Exchanges employees who help me get my manuscripts out the door in a timely fashion.

Barbara Alpert and Rose Hoenig, R.D., L.D., for helping with the more technical sides of what I do. Barbara makes sure I use the right words so you can understand what I write and Rose double-checks my ingredients so that anyone concerned with health can use my recipes with complete confidence.

Cliff Lund and everyone in my family, who support my mission of "common folk" healthy recipes and a commonsense approach to healthy living.

God, for giving me the talent to do what I do and for ensuring that both Putnam and QVC would come into my life at the right moment.

Stirring Up a Lot of Healthy Nutrition in One Tasty Kettle

Do you remember venturing into your grandma's kitchen and spotting her enormous soup kettle bubbling away on her big cookstove? Did you ever pull over a kitchen chair and try to peek into it to see what she was cooking? Oh, how those comforting aromas wafted through the entire house and made your tummy start to rumble with wishing it was time to eat!

Everybody loves soup, from thick chowders to delicate broths, soothing purees to spicy blends so chunky you ought to call them stews! Hot or cold, mild or tangy, rich with chunks of meat or brimming with all your favorite vegetables, soup is the stuff of childhood fantasies—the kind you never outgrow.

But if you think making delicious soup means spending hours over a hot stove or chopping ingredients until your hands practically fall off, I've got a surprise for you. Those old-fashioned flavors you relished when Grandma stirred them up can be yours again, but prepared the *Healthy Exchanges Way*. These soup recipes rely on healthy commercial products coupled with the best fresh ingredients. They're nowhere near as time-consuming as making soup from scratch, but you'll be thrilled to discover just how good healthy soup stirred up in a hurry can taste!

Let's play a little game of "finish the sentence" when it comes to savoring soup:

- **SOUP IS . . . filling.** And how! I recently read that people who want to lose weight should eat soup before meals because it takes the edge off hunger and helps them eat less of other, less healthy foods. Of course, this report neglected to mention that if the soup is really, really tasty, people won't only be full, they'll be truly satisfied.

- **SOUP IS . . . nourishing.** If anyone at your house is having trouble getting those five daily servings of fruits and vegetables, soup is a perfect solution! You can cook vegetables and then puree them in your blender to thicken up a pot of soup. You can also get your family to eat a variety of vegetables when they're cut up small in a bowl of soup. Imagine, not a word of argument to get a kid to eat carrots *and* string beans *and* peas at the same meal!

- **SOUP IS . . . thrifty.** I grew up in a small town and learned firsthand from my mother how smart and inexpensive it is to serve soup often. She made every bowl of soup an adventure for us, surprising us with different combinations of vegetables and leftover meats. You can cut up just about anything in your refrigerator to add to a pot of soup, especially those veggies that are about a day from being thrown out. Soup is also a great illustration of that motto about necessity being the mother of invention. (My mother certainly understood it!) Sometimes, when there isn't much left of several soups we've prepared for JO's Kitchen Cafe, I'll create a brand-new recipe that simply combines the best of everything in one delicious dish!

- **SOUP IS . . . healthy.** (You knew I'd be getting to that sooner or later, right?) Soup is good for the digestion and helps control appetite. It's easy to make it low in fat (plus you can always skim a bit of that excess fat off the top if you like) and low in calories (all those veggies, remember, and just a little bit of meat or poultry go a very long way).

- SOUP IS . . . cozy, comforting, and great served just about any way you can think of. It's the ideal appetizer for a party or a crowd; if you make it thick and hearty, you've created a great "main attraction"; if you stir it up sweet and fruity, you can even serve it for dessert! It's a tasty and terrific snack, beloved by kids of all ages, and a splendid solution for special occasions all year long!

Dear Friends,

People often ask me why I include the same general information at the beginning of all my cookbooks. If you've seen any of my other books you'll know that my "common folk" recipes are just one part of the Healthy Exchanges picture. You know that I firmly believe—and say so whenever and wherever I can— that *Healthy Exchanges is not a diet, it's a way of life!* That's why I include the story of Healthy Exchanges in every book, because I know that the tale of my struggle to lose weight and regain my health is one that speaks to the hearts of many thousands of people. And because Healthy Exchanges is not just a collection of recipes, I always include the wisdom that I've learned from my own experiences and the knowledge of the health and cooking professionals I meet. Whether it's learning about nutrition or making shopping and cooking easier, no Healthy Exchanges book would be complete without features like "A Peek into My Pantry" or "JoAnna's Ten Commandments of Successful Cooking."

Even if you've read my other books, you might still want to skim the following chapters—you never know when I'll slip in a new bit of wisdom or suggest a new product that will make your journey to health an easier and tastier one. If you're sharing this book with a friend or family member, you'll want to make sure they read the following pages before they start stirring up the recipes.

If this is the first book of mine that you've read, I want to welcome you with all my heart to the Healthy Exchanges Family. (And, of course, I'd love to hear your comments or questions. See the back of the book for my mailing address . . . or come visit if you happen to find yourself in DeWitt, Iowa—just ask anybody for directions to Healthy Exchanges!)

Jo Anna

JoAnna M. Lund and Healthy Exchanges

Food is the first invited guest to every special occasion in every family's memory scrapbook. From baptism to graduation, from weddings to wakes, food brings us together.

It wasn't always that way at our house. I used to eat alone, even when my family was there, because while they were dining on real food, I was nibbling at whatever my newest diet called for. In fact, for twenty-eight years, I called myself the diet queen of DeWitt, Iowa.

I tried every diet I ever came across, every one I could afford, and every one that found its way to my small town in eastern Iowa. I was willing to try anything that promised to "melt off the pounds," determined to deprive my body in every possible way in order to become thin at last.

I sent away for expensive "miracle" diet pills. I starved myself on the Cambridge Diet and the Bahama Diet. I gobbled diet candies, took thyroid pills, fiber pills, prescription and over-the-counter diet pills. I went to endless weight-loss support group meetings—but I somehow managed to turn healthy programs such as Overeaters Anonymous, Weight Watchers, and TOPS into unhealthy diets . . . diets I could never follow for more than a few months.

I was determined to discover something that worked long-term, but each new failure increased my desperation that I'd never find it.

5

I ate strange concoctions and rubbed on even stranger potions. I tried liquid diets. I agreed to be hypnotized. I tried reflexology and even had an acupressure device stuck in my ear!

Does my story sound a lot like yours? I'm not surprised. No wonder the weight-loss business is a billion-dollar industry!

Every new thing I tried seemed to work—at least at first. And losing that first five or ten pounds would get me so excited, I'd believe that this new miracle diet would, finally, get my weight off for keeps.

Inevitably, though, the initial excitement wore off. The diet's routine and boredom set in, and I quit. I shoved the pills to the back of the medicine chest; pushed the cans of powdered shake mix to the rear of the kitchen cabinets; slid all the program materials out of sight under my bed; and once more I felt like a failure.

Like most dieters, I quickly gained back the weight I'd lost each time, along with a few extra "souvenir" pounds that seemed always to settle around my hips. I'd done the diet-lose-weight-gain-it-all-back "yo-yo" on the average of once a year. It's no exaggeration to say that over the years I've lost 1,000 pounds—and gained back 1,150 pounds.

Finally, at the age of forty-six I weighed more than I'd ever imagined possible. I'd stopped believing that any diet could work for me. I drowned my sorrows in sacks of cake donuts and wondered if I'd live long enough to watch my grandchildren grow up.

Something had to change.

I had to change.

Finally, I did.

I'm over fifty now—and I'm 130 pounds less than my all-time high of close to 300 pounds. I've kept the weight off for more than seven years. I'd like to lose another ten pounds, but I'm not obsessed about it. If it takes me two or three years to accomplish it, that's okay.

What I *do* care about is never saying hello again to any of those unwanted pounds I said good-bye to!

How did I jump off the roller coaster I was on? For one thing, I finally stopped looking to food to solve my emotional problems. But what really shook me up—and got me started on the path that changed my life—was Operation Desert Storm in early 1991. I sent three children off to the Persian Gulf War—my son-in-law Matt, a medic in Special Forces; my daughter, Becky, a full-time college student and member of a medical unit in the Army Reserve; and my son, James, a member of the Inactive Army Reserve reactivated as a chemicals expert.

Somehow, knowing that my children were putting their lives on the line got me thinking about my own mortality—and I knew in my heart the last thing they needed while they were overseas was to get a letter from home saying that their mother was ill because of a food-related problem.

The day I drove the third child to the airport to leave for Saudi Arabia, something happened to me that would change my life for the better—and forever. I stopped praying my constant prayer as a professional dieter, which was simply "Please, God, let me lose ten pounds by Friday." Instead, I began praying, "God, please help me not to be a burden to my kids and my family." I quit praying for what I wanted and started praying for what I needed—and in the process my prayers were answered. I couldn't keep the kids safe—that was out of my hands—but I could try to get healthier to better handle the stress of it. It was the least I could do on the homefront.

That quiet prayer was the beginning of the new JoAnna Lund. My initial goal was not to lose weight or create healthy recipes. I only wanted to become healthier for my kids, my husband, and myself.

Each of my children returned safely from the Persian Gulf War. But something didn't come back—the 130 extra pounds I'd been lugging around for far too long. I'd finally accepted the truth after all those agonizing years of suffering through on-again, off-again dieting.

There are no "magic" cures in life.

No "miracle" potion, pill, or diet will make unwanted pounds disappear.

I found something better than magic, if you can believe it. When I turned my weight and health dilemma over to God for guidance, a new JoAnna Lund and Healthy Exchanges were born.

I discovered a new way to live my life—and uncovered an unexpected talent for creating easy "common folk" healthy recipes, and sharing my commonsense approach to healthy living. I learned that I could motivate others to change their lives and adopt a positive outlook. I began publishing cookbooks and a monthly food newsletter, and speaking to groups all over the country.

I like to say, "*When life handed me a lemon, not only did I make healthy, tasty lemonade, I wrote the recipe down!*"

What I finally found was not a quick fix or a short-term diet, but a great way to live well for a lifetime.

I want to share it with you.

Food Exchanges and Weight Loss Choices™

If you've ever been on one of the national weight-loss programs like Weight Watchers or Diet Center, you've already been introduced to the concept of measured portions of different food groups that make up your daily food plan. If you are not familiar with such a system of weight-loss choices or exchanges, here's a brief explanation. (If you want or need more detailed information, you can write to the American Dietetic Association or the American Diabetes Association for comprehensive explanations.)

The idea of food exchanges is to divide foods into basic food groups. The foods in each group are measured in servings that have comparable values. These groups include Proteins/Meats, Breads/Starches, Fruits, Skim Milk, Vegetables, Fats, Free Foods, and Optional Calories.

Each choice or exchange included in a particular group has about the same number of calories and a similar carbohydrate, protein, and fat content as the other foods in that group. Because any food on a particular list can be "exchanged" for any other food in that group, it makes sense to call the food groups *exchanges* or *choices.*

I like to think we are also "exchanging" bad habits and food choices for good ones!

By using Weight Loss Choices or exchanges you can choose from a variety of foods without having to calculate the nutrient value of each one. This makes it easier to include a wide variety of foods in your daily menus and gives you the opportunity to tailor your choices to your unique appetite.

If you want to lose weight, you should consult your physician or other weight-control expert regarding the number of servings that would be best for you from each food group. Since men generally require more calories than women, and since the requirements for growing children and teenagers differ from those of adults, the right number of exchanges for any one person is a personal decision.

I have included a suggested plan of weight-loss choices in the pages following the exchange lists. It's a program I used to lose 130 pounds, and it's the one I still follow today.

(If you are a diabetic or have been diagnosed with heart problems, it is best to meet with your physician before using this or any other food program or recipe collection.)

Food Group Weight Loss Choices/Exchanges

Not all food group exchanges are alike. The ones that follow are for anyone who's interested in weight loss or maintenance. If you are a diabetic, you should check with your health-care provider or dietitian to get the information you need to help you plan your diet. Diabetic exchanges are calculated by the American Diabetic Association, and information about them is provided in *The Diabetic's Healthy Exchanges Cookbook* (Perigee Books).

Every Healthy Exchanges recipe provides calculations in three ways:

- Weight Loss Choices/Exchanges

- Calories; Fat, Protein, Carbohydrates, and Fiber in grams; Sodium and Calcium in milligrams

- Diabetic Exchanges calculated for me by a registered dietitian

Healthy Exchanges recipes can help you eat well and recover your health, whatever your health concerns may be. Please take a few minutes to review the exchange lists and the suggestions that follow on how to count them. You have lots of great eating in store for you!

Proteins

Meat, poultry, seafood, eggs, cheese, and legumes. One exchange of Protein is approximately 60 calories. Examples of one Protein choice or exchange:

> 1 ounce cooked weight of lean meat, poultry, or seafood
> 2 ounces white fish
> 1½ ounces 97% fat-free ham
> 1 egg (limit to no more than 4 per week)
> ¼ cup egg substitute
> 3 egg whites
> ¾ ounce reduced-fat cheese
> ½ cup fat-free cottage cheese
> 2 ounces cooked or ¾ ounce uncooked dry beans
> 1 tablespoon peanut butter (also count 1 fat exchange)

Breads

Breads, crackers, cereals, grains, and starchy vegetables. One exchange of Bread is approximately 80 calories. Examples of one Bread choice or exchange:

> 1 slice bread or 2 slices reduced-calorie bread (40 calories or less)
> 1 roll, any type (1 ounce)
> ½ cup cooked pasta or ¾ ounce uncooked (scant ½ cup)
> ½ cup cooked rice or 1 ounce uncooked (⅓ cup)
> 3 tablespoons flour
> ¾ ounce cold cereal
> ½ cup cooked hot cereal or ¾ ounce uncooked
>   (2 tablespoons)
> ½ cup corn (kernels or cream-style) or peas
> 4 ounces white potato, cooked, or 5 ounces uncooked

3 ounces sweet potato, cooked, or 4 ounces uncooked
3 cups air-popped popcorn
7 fat-free crackers (¾ ounce)
3 (2½-inch squares) graham crackers
2 (¾-ounce) rice cakes or 6 mini
1 tortilla, any type (6-inch diameter)

Fruits

All fruits and fruit juices. One exchange of Fruit is approximately 60 calories. Examples of one Fruit choice or exchange:

1 small apple or ½ cup slices
1 small orange
½ medium banana
¾ cup berries (except strawberries and cranberries)
1 cup strawberries or cranberries
½ cup canned fruit, packed in fruit juice or rinsed well
2 tablespoons raisins
1 tablespoon spreadable fruit spread
½ cup apple juice (4 fluid ounces)
½ cup orange juice (4 fluid ounces)
½ cup applesauce

Skim Milk

Milk, buttermilk, and yogurt. One exchange of Skim Milk is approximately 90 calories. Examples of one Skim Milk choice or exchange:

1 cup skim milk
½ cup evaporated skim milk
1 cup low-fat buttermilk
¾ cup plain fat-free yogurt
⅓ cup nonfat dry milk powder

Vegetables

All fresh, canned, or frozen vegetables other than the starchy vegetables. One exchange of Vegetable is approximately 30 calories. Examples of one Vegetable choice or exchange:

> ½ *cup vegetable*
> ¼ *cup tomato sauce*
> *1 medium fresh tomato*
> ½ *cup vegetable juice*

Fats

Margarine, mayonnaise, vegetable oils, salad dressings, olives, and nuts. One exchange of Fat is approximately 40 calories. Examples of one Fat choice or exchange:

> *1 teaspoon margarine or 2 teaspoons reduced-calorie margarine*
> *1 teaspoon butter*
> *1 teaspoon vegetable oil*
> *1 teaspoon mayonnaise or 2 teaspoons reduced-calorie*
>   *mayonnaise*
> *1 teaspoon peanut butter*
> *1 ounce olives*
> ¼ *ounce pecans or walnuts*

Free Foods

Foods that do not provide nutritional value but are used to enhance the taste of foods are included in the Free Foods group. Examples of these are spices, herbs, extracts, vinegar, lemon juice, mustard, Worcestershire sauce, and soy sauce. Cooking sprays and artificial sweeteners used in moderation are also included in this group. However, you'll see that I include the caloric value of artificial sweeteners in the Optional Calories of the recipes.

You may occasionally see a recipe that lists "free food" as part of the portion. According to the published exchange lists, a free food contains fewer than 20 calories per serving. Two or three servings per day of free foods/drinks are usually allowed in a meal plan.

Optional Calories

Foods that do not fit into any other group but are used in moderation in recipes are included in Optional Calories. Foods that are counted in this way include sugar-free gelatin and puddings, fat-free mayonnaise and dressings, reduced-calorie whipped toppings, reduced-calorie syrups and jams, chocolate chips, coconut, and canned broth.

Sliders™

These are 80 Optional Calorie increments that do not fit into any particular category. You can choose which food group to *slide* these into. It is wise to limit this selection to approximately three to four per day to ensure the best possible nutrition for your body while still enjoying an occasional treat.

Sliders may be used in either of the following ways:

1. If you have consumed all your Protein, Bread, Fruit, or Skim Milk Weight Loss Choices for the day, and you want to eat additional foods from those food groups, you simply use a Slider. It's what I call "healthy horse trading." Remember that Sliders may not be traded for choices in the Vegetables or Fats food groups.

2. Sliders may also be deducted from your Optional Calories for the day or week. ¼ Slider equals 20 Optional Calories; ½ Slider equals 40 Optional Calories; ¾ Slider equals 60 Optional Calories; and 1 Slider equals 80 Optional Calories.

Healthy Exchanges Weight Loss Choices

My original Healthy Exchanges program of Weight Loss Choices
was based on an average daily total of 1,400 to 1,600 calories per
day. That was what I determined was right for my needs, and for
those of most women. Because men require additional calories
(about 1,600 to 1,900), here are my suggested plans for women
and men. (*If you require more or fewer calories, please revise this plan
to meet your individual needs.*)

Each day, women should plan to eat:

2 Skim Milk servings, 90 calories each
2 Fat servings, 40 calories each
3 Fruit servings, 60 calories each
4 Vegetable servings or more, 30 calories each
5 Protein servings, 60 calories each
5 Bread servings, 80 calories each

Each day, men should plan to eat:

2 Skim Milk servings, 90 calories each
4 Fat servings, 40 calories each
3 Fruit servings, 60 calories each
4 Vegetable servings or more, 30 calories each
6 Protein servings, 60 calories each
7 Bread servings, 80 calories each

Young people should follow the program for men but add 1
Skim Milk serving for a total of 3 servings.

You may also choose to add up to 100 Optional Calories per
day, and up to 21 to 28 Sliders per week at 80 calories each. If you
choose to include more Sliders in your daily or weekly totals,
deduct those 80 calories from your Optional Calorie "bank."
A word about **Sliders:** These are to be counted toward your

totals after you have used your allotment of choices of Skim Milk, Protein, Bread, and Fruit for the day. By "sliding" an additional choice into one of these groups, you can meet your individual needs for that day. Sliders are especially helpful when traveling, stressed-out, eating out, or for special events. I often use mine so I can enjoy my favorite Healthy Exchanges desserts. Vegetables are not to be counted as Sliders. Enjoy as many Vegetable choices as you need to feel satisfied. Because we want to limit our fat intake to moderate amounts, additional Fat choices should not be counted as Sliders. If you choose to include more fat on an *occasional* basis, count the extra choices as Optional Calories.

Keep a daily food diary of your Weight Loss Choices, checking off what you eat as you go. If, at the end of the day, your required selections are not 100 percent accounted for, but you have done the best you can, go to bed with a clear conscience. There will be days when you have ¼ Fruit or ½ Bread left over. What are you going to do—eat two slices of an orange or half a slice of bread and throw the rest out? I always say, "Nothing in life comes out exact." Just do the best you can . . . *the best you can.*

Try to drink at least eight 8-ounce glasses of water a day. Water truly is the "nectar" of good health.

As a little added insurance, I take a multivitamin each day. It's not essential, but if my day's worth of well-planned meals "bites the dust" when unexpected events intrude on my regular routine, my body still gets its vital nutrients.

The calories listed in each group of choices are averages. Some choices within each group may be higher or lower, so it's important to select a variety of different foods instead of eating the same three or four all the time.

Use your Optional Calories! They are what I call "life's little extras." They make all the difference in how you enjoy your food and appreciate the variety available to you. Yes, we can get by without them, but do you really want to? Keep in mind that you should be using all your daily Weight Loss Choices first to ensure you are getting the basics of good nutrition. But I guarantee that Optional Calories will keep you from feeling deprived—and help you reach your weight-loss goals.

Sodium, Fat, Cholesterol, and Processed Foods

*A*re Healthy Exchanges ingredients really healthy?
      When I first created Healthy Exchanges, many people asked about sodium; about whether it was necessary to calculate the percentage of fat, saturated fat, and cholesterol in a healthy diet; and about my use of processed foods in many recipes. I researched these questions as I was developing my program, so you can feel confident about using the recipes and food plan.

Sodium

Most people consume more sodium than their bodies need. The American Heart Association and the American Diabetes Association recommend limiting daily sodium intake to no more than 3,000 milligrams per day. If your doctor suggests you limit your sodium even more, then *you really must read labels.*

      Sodium is an essential nutrient and should not be completely eliminated. It helps to regulate blood volume and is needed for normal daily muscle and nerve functions. Most of us, however, have no trouble getting "all we need" and then some.

      As with everything else, moderation is my approach. I rarely ever have salt on my list as an added ingredient. But if you're especially sodium-sensitive, make the right choices for you—and save high-sodium foods such as sauerkraut for an occasional treat.

      I use lots of spices to enhance flavors, so you won't notice the absence of salt. In the few cases where it is used, salt is vital for the success of the recipe, so please don't omit it.

When I do use an ingredient high in sodium, I try to compensate by using low-sodium products in the remainder of the recipe. Many fat-free products are a little higher in sodium to make up for any loss of flavor that disappeared along with the fat. But when I take advantage of these fat-free, higher-sodium products, I stretch that ingredient within the recipe, lowering the amount of sodium per serving. A good example is my use of fat-free and reduced-sodium canned soups. While the suggested number of servings per can is two, I make sure my final creation serves at least four and sometimes six. So the soup's sodium has been "watered down" from one-third to one-half of the original amount.

Even if you don't have to watch your sodium intake for medical reasons, using moderation is another "healthy exchange" to make on your own journey to good health.

Fat Percentages

We've been told that 30 percent is the magic number—that we should limit fat intake to 30 percent or less of our total calories. It's good advice, and I try to have a weekly average of 15 percent to 25 percent myself. I believe any less than 15 percent is really just another restrictive diet that won't last. And more than 25 percent on a regular basis is too much of a good thing.

When I started listing fat grams along with calories in my recipes, I was tempted to include the percentage of calories from fat. After all, in the vast majority of my recipes, that percentage is well below 30 percent. This even includes my pie recipes that allow you a realistic serving instead of many "diet" recipes that tell you a serving is $1/12$ of a pie.

Figuring fat grams is easy enough. Each gram of fat equals 9 calories. Multiply fat grams by 9, then divide that number by the total calories to get the percentage of calories from fat.

So why don't I do it? After consulting four registered dietitians for advice, I decided to omit this information. They felt that it's too easy for people to become obsessed by that 30 percent figure, which is after all supposed to be a percentage of total calories over the course of a day or a week. We mustn't feel we can't include a healthy ingredient such as pecans or olives in one recipe just because, on its own, it has more than 30 percent of its calories from fat.

An example of this would be a casserole made with 90 percent lean red meat. Most of us benefit from eating red meat in moderation, as it provides iron and niacin in our diets, and it also makes life more enjoyable for us and those who eat with us. If we *only* look at the percentage of calories from fat in a serving of this one dish, which might be as high as 40 to 45 percent, we might choose not to include this recipe in our weekly food plan.

The dietitians suggested that it's important to consider the total picture when making such decisions. As long as your overall food plan keeps fat calories to 30 percent, it's all right to enjoy an occasional dish that is somewhat higher in fat content. Healthy foods I include in **MODERATION** include 90 percent lean red meat, olives, and nuts. I don't eat these foods every day, and you may not either. But occasionally, in a good recipe, they make all the difference in the world between just getting by (deprivation) and truly enjoying your food.

Remember, the goal is eating in a healthy way so you can enjoy and live well the rest of your life.

Saturated Fats and Cholesterol

You'll see that I don't provide calculations for saturated fats or cholesterol amounts in my recipes. It's for the simple and yet not so simple reason that accurate, up-to-date, brand-specific information can be difficult to obtain from food manufacturers, especially since the way in which they produce food keeps changing rapidly. But once more I've consulted with registered dietitians and other professionals and found that, because I use only a few products that are high in saturated fat, and use them in such limited quantities, my recipes are suitable for patients concerned about controlling or lowering cholesterol. You'll also find that whenever I do use one of these ingredients *in moderation*, everything else in the recipe, and in the meals my family and I enjoy, is low in fat.

Processed Foods

Just what *is* processed food, anyway? What do I mean by the term "processed foods," and why do I use them, when the "purest" recipe developers in Recipe Land consider them "pedestrian" and won't ever use something from a box, container, or can? A letter I received and a passing statement from a stranger made me reflect on what I mean when I refer to processed foods, and helped me reaffirm why I use them in my "common folk" healthy recipes.

If you are like the vast millions who agree with me, then I'm not sharing anything new with you. And if you happen to disagree, that's okay, too.

A few months ago, a woman sent me several articles from various "whole food" publications and wrote that she was wary of processed foods, and wondered why I used them in my recipes. She then scribbled on the bottom of her note, "Just how healthy *is* Healthy Exchanges?" Then, a few weeks later, during a chance visit at a public food event with a very pleasant woman, I was struck by how we all have our own definitions of what processed foods are. She shared with me, in a somewhat self-righteous manner, that she *never* uses processed foods. She only cooked with fresh fruits and vegetables, she told me. Then later she said that she used canned reduced-fat soups all the time! Was her definition different than mine, I wondered? Soup in a can, whether it's reduced in fat or not, still meets my definition of a processed food.

So I got out a copy of my book *HELP: Healthy Exchanges Lifetime Plan* and reread what I had written back then about processed foods. Nothing in my definition had changed since I wrote that section. I still believe that healthy processed foods, such as canned soups, prepared piecrusts, sugar-free instant puddings, fat-free sour cream, and frozen whipped topping, when used properly, all have a place as ingredients in healthy recipes.

I never use an ingredient that hasn't been approved by either the American Diabetic Association, the American Dietetic Association, or the American Heart Association. Whenever I'm in doubt, I send for their position papers, then ask knowledgeable registered dietitians to explain those papers to me in layman's language. I've been assured by all of them that the sugar- and fat-free products I use in my recipes are indeed safe.

If you don't agree, nothing I can say or write will convince you otherwise. But, if you've been using the healthy processed foods and have been concerned about the almost daily hoopla you hear about yet another product that's going to be the doom of all of us, then just stick with reason. For every product on the grocery shelves, there are those who want you to buy it and there are those who don't, *because they want you to buy their products instead.* So we have to learn to sift the fact from the fiction. Let's take sugar substitutes, for example. In making your own evaluations, you should be skeptical about any information provided by the sugar substitute manufacturers, because they have a vested interest in our buying their products. Likewise, ignore any information provided by the sugar industry, because they have a vested interest in our *not* buying sugar substitutes. Then, if you aren't sure if you can really trust the government or any of its agencies, toss out their data, too. That leaves the three associations I mentioned earlier. Do you think any of them would say a product is safe if it isn't? Or say a product isn't safe when it is? They have nothing to gain or lose, *other than their integrity*, if they intentionally try to mislead us. That's why I only go to these associations for information concerning healthy processed foods.

I certainly don't recommend that everything we eat should come from a can, box, or jar. I think the best of all possible worlds is to start with the basics: grains such as rice, pasta, or corn. Then, for example, add some raw vegetables and extra-lean meat such as poultry, fish, beef, or pork. Stir in some healthy canned soup or tomato sauce, and you'll end up with something that is not only healthy but tastes so good, everyone from toddlers to great-grandparents will want to eat it!

I've never been in favor of spraying everything we eat with chemicals, and I don't believe that all our foods should come out of packages. But I do think we should use the best available healthy processed foods to make cooking easier and food taste better. I take advantage of the good-tasting low-fat and low-sugar products found in any grocery store. My recipes are created for busy people like me, people who want to eat healthily and economically but who still want the food to satisfy their taste buds. I don't expect anyone to visit out-of-the-way health food stores or find the time to cook beans from scratch—*because I don't!* Most of you can't grow fresh food in the backyard and many of you may not have access to farmers' markets or large supermarkets. I want to help you figure out realistic ways to make healthy eating a reality *wherever you live*, or you will not stick to a healthy lifestyle for long.

So if you've been swayed (by individuals or companies with vested interests or hidden agendas) into thinking that all processed foods are bad for you, you may want to reconsider your position. Or if you've been fooling yourself into believing that you *never* use processed foods but regularly reach for that healthy canned soup, stop playing games with yourself—you are using processed foods in a healthy way. And, if you're like me and use healthy processed foods in *moderation*, don't let anyone make you feel ashamed about including these products in your healthy lifestyle. Only *you* can decide what's best for *you* and your family's needs.

Part of living a healthy lifestyle is making those decisions and then getting on with life. Congratulations on choosing to live a healthy lifestyle, and let's celebrate together by sharing a piece of Healthy Exchanges pie that I've garnished with Cool Whip Lite!

JoAnna's Ten Commandments of Successful Cooking

A very important part of any journey is knowing where you are going and the best way to get there. If you plan and prepare before you start to cook, you should reach mealtime with foods to write home about!

1. **Read the entire recipe from start to finish** and be sure you understand the process involved. Check that you have all the equipment you will need *before* you begin.

2. **Check the ingredient list** and be sure you have *everything* and in the amounts required. Keep cooking sprays handy—while they're not listed as ingredients, I use them all the time (just a quick squirt!).

3. **Set out *all* the ingredients and equipment needed** to prepare the recipe on the counter near you *before* you start. Remember that old saying *A stitch in time saves nine?* It applies in the kitchen, too.

4. **Do as much advance preparation as possible** before actually cooking. Chop, cut, grate, or do whatever is needed to prepare the ingredients and have them ready

before you start to mix. Turn the oven on at least ten minutes before putting food in to bake, to allow the oven to preheat to the proper temperature.

5. **Use a kitchen timer** to tell you when the cooking or baking time is up. Because stove temperatures vary slightly by manufacturer, you may want to set your timer for five minutes less than the suggested time just to prevent overcooking. Check the progress of your dish at that time, then decide if you need the additional minutes or not.

6. **Measure carefully.** Use glass measures for liquids and metal or plastic cups for dry ingredients. My recipes are based on standard measurements. Unless I tell you it's a scant or full cup, measure the cup level.

7. **For best results, follow the recipe instructions exactly.** Feel free to substitute ingredients that *don't tamper* with the basic chemistry of the recipe, but be sure to leave key ingredients alone. For example, you could substitute sugar-free instant chocolate pudding for sugar-free instant butterscotch pudding, but if you use a six-serving package when a four-serving package is listed in the ingredients, or you use instant when cook-and-serve is required, you won't get the right result.

8. **Clean up as you go.** It is much easier to wash a few items at a time than to face a whole counter of dirty dishes later. The same is true for spills on the counter or floor.

9. **Be careful about doubling or halving a recipe.** Though many recipes can be altered successfully to serve more or fewer people, *many cannot.* This is especially true when it comes to spices and liquids. If you try to double a recipe that calls for 1 teaspoon pumpkin pie spice, for example, and you double the spice, you may end up with a too-spicy taste. I usually suggest increasing spices or liquid by 1½ times when doubling a recipe. If it tastes a little bland to you, you can increase the spice to 1¾ times the original amount the next time you prepare the dish. Remember: You can always add more, but you can't take it out after it's stirred in.

The same is true with liquid ingredients. If you wanted to **triple** a recipe like my **Cliff's Taco Soup** because you were planning to serve a crowd, you might think you should use three times as much of every ingredient. Don't, or you could end up with Cliff's Really Soupy Taco Soup! The original recipe calls for 1 cup tomato sauce, so I'd suggest using 2 cups when you **triple** the recipe (or 1½ cups if you **double** it). You'll still have a good-tasting dish that won't overflow the bowl.

10. **Write your reactions next to each recipe once you've served it.** Yes, that's right, I'm giving you permission to write in this book. It's yours, after all. Ask yourself: Did everyone like it? Did you have to add another half teaspoon of chili seasoning to please your family, who like to live on the spicier side of the street? You may even want to rate the recipe on a scale of 1★ to 4★, depending on what you thought of it. (Four stars would be the top rating—and I hope you'll feel that way about many of my recipes.) Jotting down your comments while they are fresh in your mind will help you personalize the recipe to your own taste the next time you prepare it.

My Best Healthy Exchanges Tips and Tidbits

Measurements, General Cooking Tips, and Basic Ingredients

Sugar Substitutes

The word **moderation** best describes **my use of fats, sugar substitutes,** and **sodium** in these recipes. Wherever possible, I've used cooking spray for sautéing and for browning meats and vegetables. I also use reduced-calorie margarine and fat-free mayonnaise and salad dressings. Lean ground turkey *or* ground beef can be used in the recipes. Just be sure whatever you choose is at least *90 percent lean.*

I've also included **small amounts of sugar substitutes as the sweetening agent** in many of the recipes. I don't drink a hundred cans of soda a day or eat enough artificially sweetened foods in a 24-hour time period to be troubled by sugar substitutes. But if this is a concern of yours and you *do not* need to watch your sugar intake, you can always replace the sugar substitutes with processed sugar and the sugar-free products with regular ones.

I created my recipes knowing they would also be used by hypo-glycemics, diabetics, and those concerned about triglycerides. If you choose to use sugar instead, be sure to count the additional calories.

A word of caution when cooking with **sugar substitutes**: Use **saccharin**-based sweeteners when **heating or baking**. In recipes that **don't require heat, aspartame** (known as NutraSweet) works well in uncooked dishes but leaves an aftertaste in baked products. **Sugar Twin** is my first choice for a sugar substitute. If you can't find that, use **Sprinkle Sweet**. They measure like sugar, you can cook and bake with them, they're inexpensive, and they are easily poured from their boxes.

Many of my recipes for quick breads, muffins, and cakes include a package of sugar-free instant pudding mix, which is sweetened with NutraSweet. Yet we've been told that NutraSweet breaks down under heat. I've tested my recipes again and again, and here's what I've found: baking with a NutraSweet product sold for home sweetening doesn't work, but baking with NutraSweet-sweetened instant pudding mixes turns out great. I choose not to question why this is, but continue to use these products in creating my Healthy Exchanges recipes.

How much sweetener is the right amount? I use pourable Sugar Twin, Brown Sugar Twin, and Sprinkle Sweet in my recipes because they measure just like sugar. What could be easier? I also use them because they work wonderfully in cooked and baked products.

If you are using a brand other than these, you need to check the package to figure out how much of your sweetener will equal what's called for in the recipe.

If you choose to use real sugar or brown sugar, then you would use the same amount the recipe lists for pourable Sugar Twin or Brown Sugar Twin.

You'll see that I list specific brands only when the recipe preparation involves heat. In a salad or other recipe that doesn't require cooking, I will list the ingredient as "sugar substitute to equal 2 tablespoons sugar." You can then use any sweetener you choose—Equal, Sweet 'n Low, Sweet Ten, or any other aspartame-based sugar substitute. Just check the label so you'll be using the right amount to equal those 2 tablespoons of sugar. Or if you choose, you can use regular sugar.

With Healthy Exchanges recipes, the "sweet life" is the only life for me!

Pan Sizes

I'm often asked why I use an **8-by-8-inch baking dish** in my recipes. It's for portion control. If the recipe says it serves 4, just cut down the center, turn the dish, and cut again. Like magic, there's your serving. Also, if this is the only recipe you are preparing requiring an oven, the square dish fits into a tabletop toaster oven easily and energy can be conserved.

While many of my recipes call for an 8-by-8-inch baking dish, others ask for a 9-by-9-inch cake pan. If you don't have a 9-inch-square pan, is it all right to use your 8-inch dish instead? In most cases, the small difference in the size of these two pans won't significantly affect the finished product, so until you can get your hands on the right size pan, go ahead and use your baking dish.

However, since the 8-inch dish is usually made of glass, and the 9-inch cake pan is made of metal, you will want to adjust the baking temperature. If you're using a glass baking dish in a recipe that calls for a 9-inch pan, be sure to lower your baking temperature by 15 degrees *or* check your finished product at least 6 to 8 minutes before the specified baking time is over.

But it really is worthwhile to add a 9-by-9-inch pan to your collection, and if you're going to be baking lots of my Healthy Exchanges cakes, you'll definitely use it a lot. A cake baked in this pan will have a better texture, and the servings will be a little larger. Just think of it—an 8-by-8-inch pan produces 64 square inches of dessert, while a 9-by-9-inch pan delivers 81 square inches. Those 17 extra inches are too tasty to lose!

To make life even easier, **whenever a recipe calls for ounce measurements** (other than raw meats) I've included the closest cup equivalent. I need to use my scale daily when creating recipes, so I've measured for you at the same time.

Freezing Leftovers

Most of the recipes are for **4 to 8 servings.** If you don't have that many to feed, do what I do: freeze individual portions. Then all you have to do is choose something from the freezer and take it to work for lunch or have your evening meals prepared in advance for the week. In this way, I always have something on hand that is both good to eat and good for me.

Unless a recipe includes hard-boiled eggs, cream cheese, mayonnaise, or a raw vegetable or fruit, **the leftovers should freeze well**. (I've marked recipes that freeze well with the symbol of a **snowflake** ❄.) This includes most of the cream pies. Divide any recipe into individual servings and freeze for your own TV dinners.

Another good idea is **cutting leftover pie into individual pieces and freezing each one separately** in a small Ziploc freezer bag. Once you've cut the pie into portions, place them on a cookie sheet and put it in the freezer for 15 minutes. That way, the creamy topping won't get smashed and your pie will keep its shape.

When you want to thaw a piece of pie for yourself, you don't have to thaw the whole pie. You can practice portion control at the same time, and it works really well for brown-bag lunches. Just pull a piece out of the freezer on your way to work and by lunchtime you will have a wonderful dessert waiting for you.

Why do I so often recommend freezing leftover desserts? One reason is that if you leave baked goods made with sugar substitute out on the counter for more than a day or two, they get moldy. Sugar is a preservative and retards the molding process. It's actually what's called an antimicrobial agent, meaning it works against microbes such as molds, bacteria, fungi, and yeasts that grow in foods and can cause food poisoning. Both sugar and salt work as antimicrobial agents to withdraw water from food. Since microbes can't grow without water, food protected in this way doesn't spoil.

So what do we do if we don't want our muffins to turn moldy, but we also don't want to use sugar because of the excess carbohydrates and calories? Freeze them! Just place each muffin or individually sliced bread serving into a Ziploc sandwich bag, seal, and toss into your freezer. Then, whenever you want one for a snack or a meal, you can choose to let it thaw naturally or "zap" it in the microwave. If you know that baked goods will be eaten within a day or two, packaging them in a sealed plastic container and storing in the refrigerator will do the trick.

Unless I specify "**covered**" **for simmering or baking,** prepare my recipes **uncovered**. Occasionally you will read a recipe that asks you to cover a dish for a time, then to uncover, so read the directions carefully to avoid confusion—and to get the best results.

Cooking Spray

Low-fat cooking spray is another blessing in a Healthy Exchanges kitchen. It's currently available in three flavors . . .

- **OLIVE OIL–FLAVORED** when cooking Mexican, Italian, or Greek dishes
- **BUTTER-FLAVORED** when the hint of butter is desired
- **REGULAR** for everything else.

A quick spray of butter-flavored makes air-popped popcorn a low-fat taste treat, or try it as a butter substitute on steaming hot corn on the cob. One light spray of the skillet when browning meat will convince you that you're using "old-fashioned fat," and a quick coating of the casserole dish before you add the ingredients will make serving easier and cleanup quicker.

Baking Times

Sometimes I give you a range as a **baking time**, such as 22 to 28 minutes. Why? Because every kitchen, every stove, and every chef's cooking technique is slightly different. On a hot and humid day in Iowa, the optimum cooking time won't be the same as on a cold, dry day. Some stoves bake hotter than the temperature setting indicates; other stoves bake cooler. Electric ovens are usually more temperamental than gas ovens. If you place your baking pan on a lower shelf, the temperature is warmer than if you place it on a higher shelf. If you stir the mixture more vigorously than I do, you could affect the required baking time by a minute or more.

The best way to gauge the heat of your particular oven is to purchase an oven temperature gauge that hangs in the oven. These can be found in any discount store or kitchen equipment store, and if you're going to be cooking and baking regularly, it's a good idea to own one. Set the oven to 350 degrees and when the oven indicates that it has reached that temperature, check the reading on the gauge. If it's less than 350 degrees, you know your oven cooks cooler, and you need to add a few minutes to the cooking time *or* set your oven at a higher temperature. If it's more than 350 degrees, then your oven is warmer and you need to subtract a few minutes from the cooking time. In any event, always treat the suggested baking time as approximate. Check on your baked product at the earliest suggested time. You can always continue baking a few minutes more if needed, but you can't unbake it once you've cooked it too long.

Miscellaneous Ingredients/Tips

I use reduced-sodium **canned chicken broth** in place of dry bouillon to lower the sodium content. The intended flavor is still present in the prepared dish. As a reduced-sodium beef broth is not currently available (at least not in DeWitt, Iowa), I use the canned regular beef broth. The sodium content is still lower than regular dry bouillon.

Whenever **cooked rice or pasta** is an ingredient, follow the package directions, but eliminate the salt and/or margarine called for. This helps lower the sodium and fat content. It tastes just fine; trust me on this.

Here's another tip: When **cooking rice or noodles**, why not cook extra "for the pot"? After you use what you need, store leftover rice in a covered container (where it will keep for a couple of days). With noodles like spaghetti or macaroni, first rinse and drain as usual, then measure out what you need. Put the leftovers in a bowl covered with water, then store in the refrigerator, covered, until they're needed. Then, measure out what you need, rinse and drain them, and they're ready to go.

Does your **pita bread** often tear before you can make a sandwich? Here's my tip to make them open easily: cut the bread in half, put the halves in the microwave for about 15 seconds, and they will open up by themselves. *Voilà!*

When **chunky salsa** is listed as an ingredient, I leave the degree of "heat" up to your personal taste. In our house, I'm considered a wimp. I go for the "mild" while Cliff prefers "extra-hot." How do we compromise? I prepare the recipe with mild salsa because he can always add a spoonful or two of the hotter version to his serving, but I can't enjoy the dish if it's too spicy for me.

Milk, Yogurt, and More

Take it from me—nonfat dry milk powder is great! I *do not* use it for drinking, but I *do* use it for cooking. Three good reasons why:

1. It is very **inexpensive**.

2. It does not **sour** because you use it only as needed. Store the box in your refrigerator or freezer and it will keep almost forever.

3. You can easily **add extra calcium** to just about any recipe without added liquid.

I consider nonfat dry milk powder one of Mother Nature's modern-day miracles of convenience. But do purchase a good national name brand (I like Carnation) and keep it fresh by proper storage.

I've said many times, "Give me my mixing bowl, my wire whisk, and a box of nonfat dry milk powder, and I can conquer the world!" Here are some of my favorite ways to use dry milk powder:

1. You can make a **pudding** with the nutrients of 2 cups skim milk, but the liquid of only 1¼ to 1½ cups by using ⅔ cup nonfat dry milk powder, a 4-serving package of sugar-free instant pudding, and the lesser amount of water. This makes the pudding taste much creamier and more like homemade. Also, pie filling made my way will set up in minutes. If company is knocking at your door, you can prepare a pie for them almost as fast as you can open the door and invite them in. And if by chance you have leftovers, the filling will not separate the way it does when you use the 2 cups skim milk suggested on the package. (If you absolutely refuse to use this handy powdered milk, you can substitute skim milk in the amount of water I call for. Your pie won't be as creamy, and will likely get runny if you have leftovers.)

2. You can make your own **"sour cream"** by combining ¾ cup plain fat-free yogurt with ⅓ cup nonfat dry milk powder. What you did by doing this is fourfold: (1) The dry milk stabilizes the yogurt and keeps the whey from separating. (2) The dry milk slightly helps to cut the tartness of the yogurt. (3) It's still virtually fat-free. (4) The calcium has been increased by 100 percent. Isn't it great how we can make that distant relative of sour cream a first kissin' cousin by adding the nonfat dry milk powder? Or, if you

place 1 cup plain fat-free yogurt in a sieve lined with a coffee filter, and place the sieve over a small bowl and refrigerate for about 6 hours, you will end up with a very good alternative for sour cream. To **stabilize yogurt** when cooking or baking with it, just add 1 teaspoon cornstarch to every ¾ cup yogurt.

3. You can make **evaporated skim milk** by using ⅓ cup nonfat dry milk powder and ½ cup water for every ½ cup evaporated skim milk you need. This is handy to know when you want to prepare a recipe calling for evaporated skim milk and you don't have any in the cupboard. And if you are using a recipe that requires only 1 cup evaporated skim milk, you don't have to worry about what to do with the leftover milk in the can.

4. You can make **sugar-free and fat-free sweetened condensed milk** by using 1⅓ cups nonfat dry milk powder mixed with ½ cup cold water, microwaved on HIGH until the mixture is hot but not boiling. Then stir in ½ cup Sprinkle Sweet or pourable Sugar Twin. Cover and chill at least 4 hours.

5. For any recipe that calls for **buttermilk,** you might want to try **JO's Buttermilk**: Blend 1 cup water and ⅔ cup nonfat dry milk powder (the nutrients of 2 cups of skim milk). It'll be thicker than this mixed-up milk usually is, because it's doubled. Add 1 teaspoon white vinegar and stir, then let it sit for at least 10 minutes.

What else? Nonfat dry milk powder adds calcium without fuss to many recipes, and it can be stored for months in your refrigerator or freezer.

Soup Substitutes

One of my subscribers was looking for a way to further restrict salt intake and needed a substitute for **cream of mushroom soup**. For many of my recipes, I use Healthy Request Cream of Mushroom Soup, as it is a reduced-sodium product. The label suggests two servings per can, but I usually incorporate the soup into a recipe serving at least four. By doing this, I've reduced the sodium in the soup by half again.

But if you must restrict your sodium even more, try making my Healthy Exchanges **Creamy Mushroom Sauce.** Place 1½ cups evaporated skim milk and 3 tablespoons flour in a covered jar. Shake well and pour the mixture into a medium saucepan sprayed with butter-flavored cooking spray. Add ½ cup canned sliced mushrooms, rinsed and drained. Cook over medium heat, stirring often, until the mixture thickens. Add any seasonings of your choice. You can use this sauce in any recipe that calls for one 10¾-ounce can of cream of mushroom soup.

Why did I choose these proportions and ingredients?

- 1½ cups evaporated skim milk is the amount in one can.

- It's equal to three Skim Milk choices or exchanges.

- It's the perfect amount of liquid and flour for a medium cream sauce.

- 3 tablespoons flour is equal to one Bread/Starch choice or exchange.

- Any leftovers will reheat beautifully with a flour-based sauce, but not with a cornstarch base.

- The mushrooms are one Vegetable choice or exchange.

- This sauce is virtually fat-free, sugar-free, and sodium-free.

Proteins

Eggs

I use eggs in moderation. I enjoy the real thing on an average of three to four times a week. So, my recipes are calculated on using whole eggs. However, if you choose to use egg substitute in place of the egg, the finished product will turn out just fine and the fat grams per serving will be even lower than those listed.

If you like the look, taste, and feel of **hard-boiled eggs** in salads but haven't been using them because of the cholesterol in the yolk, I have a couple of alternatives for you. (1) Pour an 8-ounce carton of egg substitute into a medium skillet sprayed with cooking spray. Cover the skillet tightly and cook over low heat until the substitute is just set, about 10 minutes. Remove from heat and let set, still covered, for 10 minutes more. Uncover and cool completely. Chop the set mixture. This will make about 1 cup of chopped egg. (2) Even easier is to hard-boil "real eggs," toss the yolk away, and chop the white. Either way, you don't deprive yourself of the pleasure of egg in your salad.

In most recipes calling for **egg substitutes**, you can use 2 egg whites in place of the equivalent of 1 egg substitute. Just break the eggs open and toss the yolks away. I can hear some of you already saying, "But that's wasteful!" Well, take a look at the price on the egg substitute package (which usually has the equivalent of 4 eggs in it), then look at the price of a dozen eggs, from which you'd get the equivalent of 6 egg substitutes. Now, what's wasteful about that?

Meats

Whenever I include **cooked chicken** in a recipe, I use roasted white meat without skin. Whenever I include **roast beef or pork** in a recipe, I use the loin cuts because they are much leaner. However, most of the time, I do my roasting of all these meats at the local deli. I just ask for a chunk of their lean roasted meat, 6 or 8 ounces, and ask them not to slice it. When I get home, I cube or dice the meat and am ready to use it in my recipe. The reason I do this is threefold: (1) I'm getting just the amount I need without leftovers; (2) I don't have the expense of heating the oven; and (3) I'm not throwing away the bone, gristle, and fat I'd be cutting off the meat. Overall, it is probably cheaper to "roast" it the way I do.

Did you know that you can make an acceptable meatloaf without using egg for the binding? Just replace every egg with ¼ cup of liquid. You could use beef broth, tomato sauce, even applesauce, to name just a few. For a meatloaf to serve 6, I always use 1 pound of extra-lean ground beef or turkey, 6 tablespoons of dried fine bread crumbs, and ¼ cup of the liquid, plus anything else healthy that strikes my fancy at the time. I mix well and place the mixture in an 8-by-8-inch baking dish or 9-by-5-inch loaf pan sprayed with cooking spray. Bake uncovered at 350 degrees for 35 to 50 minutes (depending on the added ingredients). You will never miss the egg.

Any time you are **browning ground meat** for a casserole and want to get rid of almost all the excess fat, just place the uncooked meat loosely in a plastic colander. Set the colander in a glass pie plate. Place in the microwave and cook on HIGH for 3 to 6 minutes (depending on the amount being browned), stirring often. Use as you would for any casserole. You can also chop up onions and brown them with the meat if you want.

Gravy

For **gravy** with all the "old time" flavor but without the extra fat, try this almost effortless way to prepare it. (It's almost as easy as opening up a store-bought jar.) Pour the juice off your roasted meat, then set the roast aside to "rest" for about 20 minutes. Place the juice in an uncovered cake pan or other large flat pan (we want the large air surface to speed up the cooling process) and put in the freezer until the fat congeals on top and you can skim it off. Or, if you prefer, use a skimming pitcher purchased at your kitchen gadget store. Either way, measure about 1½ cups skimmed broth and pour into a medium saucepan. Cook over medium heat until heated through, about 5 minutes. In a covered jar, combine ½ cup water or cooled potato broth with 3 tablespoons flour. Shake well. Pour the flour mixture into the warmed juice. Combine well using a wire whisk. Continue cooking until the gravy thickens, about 5 minutes. Season with salt and pepper to taste.

Why did I use flour instead of cornstarch? Because any leftovers will reheat nicely with the flour base and would not with a cornstarch base. Also, 3 tablespoons of flour works out to 1 Bread/Starch exchange. This virtually fat-free gravy makes about 2 cups, so you could spoon about ½ cup gravy on your low-fat mashed potatoes and only have to count your gravy as ¼ Bread/Starch exchange.

Fruits and Vegetables

If you want to enjoy a **"fruit shake"** with some pizzazz, just combine soda water and unsweetened fruit juice in a blender. Add crushed ice. Blend on HIGH until thick. Refreshment without guilt.

You'll see that many recipes use ordinary **canned vegetables.** They're much cheaper than reduced-sodium versions, and once you rinse and drain them, the sodium is reduced anyway. I believe in saving money wherever possible so we can afford the best fat-free and sugar-free products as they come onto the market.

All three kinds of **vegetables—fresh, frozen, and canned—** have their place in a healthy diet. My husband, Cliff, hates the taste of frozen or fresh green beans, thinks the texture is all wrong, so I use canned green beans instead. In this case, canned vegetables have their proper place when I'm feeding my husband. If someone in your family has a similar concern, it's important to respond to it so everyone can be happy and enjoy the meal.

When I use **fruits or vegetables** like apples, cucumbers, and zucchini, I wash them really well and **leave the skin on.** It provides added color, fiber, and attractiveness to any dish. And, because I use processed flour in my cooking, I like to increase the fiber in my diet by eating my fruits and vegetables in their closest-to-natural state.

To help keep **fresh fruits and veggies fresh**, just give them a quick "shower" with lemon juice. The easiest way to do this is to pour purchased lemon juice into a kitchen spray bottle and store in the refrigerator. Then, every time you use fresh fruits or vegetables in a salad or dessert, simply give them a quick spray with your "lemon spritzer." You just might be amazed by how this little trick keeps your produce from turning brown so fast.

The next time you warm canned vegetables such as carrots or green beans, drain and heat the vegetables in ¼ cup beef or chicken broth. It gives a nice variation to an old standby. Here's a simple **white sauce** for vegetables and casseroles without added fat that can be made by spraying a medium saucepan with butter-flavored cooking spray. Place 1½ cups evaporated skim milk and 3 tablespoons flour in a covered jar. Shake well. Pour into the sprayed saucepan and cook over medium heat until thick, stirring constantly. Add salt and pepper to taste. You can also add ½ cup canned drained mushrooms and/or 3 ounces (¾ cup) shredded reduced-fat cheese. Continue cooking until the cheese melts.

Zip up canned or frozen green beans with **chunky salsa**: ½ cup salsa to 2 cups beans. Heat thoroughly. Chunky salsa also makes a wonderful dressing on lettuce salads. It only counts as a vegetable, so enjoy.

Another wonderful **South of the Border** dressing can be stirred up by using ½ cup of chunky salsa and ¼ cup fat-free ranch dressing. Cover and store in your refrigerator. Use as a dressing for salads or as a topping for baked potatoes.

Delightful Dessert Ideas

For a special treat that tastes anything but "diet," try placing **spreadable fruit** in a container and microwave for about 15 seconds. Then pour the melted fruit spread over a serving of nonfat ice cream or frozen yogurt. One tablespoon of spreadable fruit is equal to 1 Fruit choice or exchange. Some combinations to get you started are apricot over chocolate ice cream, strawberry over strawberry ice cream, or any flavor over vanilla.

Another way I use spreadable fruit is to make a delicious **topping for a cheesecake or angel food cake**. I take ½ cup fruit and ½ cup Cool Whip Lite and blend the two together with a teaspoon of coconut extract.

Here's a really **good topping** for the fall of the year. Place 1½ cups unsweetened applesauce in a medium saucepan or 4-cup glass measure. Stir in 2 tablespoons raisins, 1 teaspoon apple pie spice, and 2 tablespoons Cary's Sugar Free Maple Syrup. Cook over medium heat on the stovetop or microwave on HIGH until warm. Then spoon about ½ cup of the warm mixture over pancakes, French toast, or sugar- and fat-free vanilla ice cream. It's as close as you will get to guilt-free apple pie!

Do you love hot fudge sundaes as much as I do? Here's my secret for making **Almost Sinless Hot Fudge Sauce**. Just combine the contents of a 4-serving package of JELL-O sugar-free chocolate cook-and-serve pudding with ⅔ cup Carnation Nonfat Dry Milk Powder in a medium saucepan. Add 1¼ cups water. Cook over medium heat, stirring constantly with a wire whisk, until the mixture thickens and starts to boil. Remove from heat and stir in 1 teaspoon vanilla extract, 2 teaspoons reduced-calorie margarine, and ½ cup miniature marshmallows. This makes six ¼-cup servings. Any leftovers can be refrigerated and reheated later in the microwave. Yes, you can buy fat-free chocolate syrup nowadays, but have you checked the sugar content? For a ¼-cup serving of store-bought syrup (and you show me any true hot fudge sundae lover who would settle for less than ¼ cup) it clocks in at over 150 calories with 39 grams of sugar! Hershey's Lite

Syrup, while better, still has 100 calories and 10 grams of sugar. But this "homemade" version costs you only 60 calories, less than ½ gram of fat, and just 6 grams of sugar for the same ¼-cup serving. For an occasional squirt on something where 1 teaspoon is enough, I'll use Hershey's Lite Syrup. But when I crave a hot fudge sundae, I scoop out some sugar- and fat-free ice cream, then spoon my Almost Sinless Hot Fudge Sauce over the top and smile with pleasure.

A quick yet tasty way to prepare **strawberries for shortcake** is to place about ¾ cup sliced strawberries, 2 tablespoons Diet Mountain Dew, and sugar substitute to equal ¼ cup sugar in a blender container. Process on BLEND until the mixture is smooth. Pour the mixture into a bowl. Add 1¼ cups sliced strawberries and mix well. Cover and refrigerate until ready to serve with shortcakes. This tastes just like the strawberry sauce I remember my mother making when I was a child.

Have you tried **thawing Cool Whip Lite** by stirring it? Don't! You'll get a runny mess and ruin the look and taste of your dessert. You can *never* treat Cool Whip Lite the same way you did regular Cool Whip because the "lite" version just doesn't contain enough fat. Thaw your Cool Whip Lite by placing it in your refrigerator at least two hours before you need to use it. When they took the excess fat out of Cool Whip to make it "lite," they replaced it with air. When you stir the living daylights out of it to hurry up the thawing, you also stir out the air. You also can't thaw your Cool Whip Lite in the microwave, or you'll end up with Cool Whip Soup!

Always have a thawed container of Cool Whip Lite in your refrigerator, as it keeps well for up to two weeks. It actually freezes and thaws and freezes and thaws again quite well, so if you won't be using it soon, you could refreeze your leftovers. Just remember to take it out a few hours before you need it, so it'll be creamy and soft and ready to use.

Remember, anytime you see the words "fat-free" or "reduced-fat" on the labels of cream cheese, sour cream, or whipped topping, handle it gently. The fat has been replaced by air or water, and the product has to be treated with special care.

How can you **frost an entire pie with just ½ cup of whipped topping?** First, don't use an inexpensive brand. I use Cool Whip Lite or La Creme Lite. Make sure the topping is fully thawed. Always spread from the center to the sides using a rubber spatula. This way,

½ cup topping will cover an entire pie. Remember, the operative word is *frost*, not pile the entire container on top of the pie!

Another trick I often use is to include tiny amounts of "real people" food, such as coconut, but extend the flavor by using extracts. Try it—you will be surprised by how little of the real thing you can use and still feel you are not being deprived.

If you are preparing a pie filling that has ample moisture, just line the bottom of a 9-by-9-inch cake pan with **graham crackers**. Pour the filling over the top of the crackers. Cover and refrigerate until the moisture has enough time to soften the crackers. Overnight is best. This eliminates the added **fats and sugars of a piecrust.**

One of my readers provided a smart and easy way to enjoy a **two-crust pie** without all the fat that usually comes along with those two crusts. Just use one Pillsbury refrigerated piecrust. Let it set at room temperature for about 20 minutes. Cut the crust in half on the folded line. Gently roll each half into a ball. Wipe your counter with a wet cloth and place a sheet of wax paper on it. Put one of the balls on the wax paper, then cover with another piece of wax paper, and roll it out with your rolling pin. Carefully remove the wax paper on one side and place that side into your 8- or 9-inch pie plate. Fill with your usual pie filling, then repeat the process for the top crust. Bake as usual. Enjoy!

When you are preparing a pie that uses a purchased piecrust, simply tear out the paper label on the plastic cover (but do check it for a coupon good on a future purchase) and turn the cover upside down over the prepared pie. You now have a cover that protects your beautifully garnished pie from having anything fall on top of it. It makes the pie very portable when it's your turn to bring dessert to a get-together.

Did you know you can make your own **fruit-flavored yogurt?** Mix 1 tablespoon of any flavor of spreadable fruit spread with ¾ cup plain yogurt. It's every bit as tasty and much cheaper. You can also make your own **lemon yogurt** by combining 3 cups plain fat-free yogurt with 1 tub Crystal Light lemonade powder. Mix well, cover, and store in the refrigerator. I think you will be pleasantly surprised by the ease, cost, and flavor of this "made from scratch" calcium-rich treat. P.S.: You can make any flavor you like by using any of the Crystal Light mixes—Cranberry? Iced Tea? You decide.

Other Smart Substitutions

Many people have inquired about **substituting applesauce and artificial sweetener for butter and sugar**, but what if you aren't satisfied with the result? One woman wrote to me about a recipe for her grandmother's cookies that called for 1 cup of butter and 1½ cups of sugar. Well, any recipe that depends on as much butter and sugar as this one does is generally not a good candidate for "healthy exchanges." The original recipe needed a large quantity of fat to produce a crisp cookie just like Grandma made.

Applesauce can often be used instead of vegetable oil, but generally doesn't work well as a replacement for butter, margarine, or lard. If a recipe calls for ½ cup of vegetable oil or less and your recipe is for a bar cookie, quick bread, muffin, or cake mix, you can try substituting an equal amount of unsweetened applesauce. If the recipe calls for more, try using ½ cup applesauce and the rest oil. You're cutting down the fat but shouldn't end up with a taste disaster! This "applesauce shortening" works great in many recipes, but so far I haven't been able to figure out a way to deep-fat fry with it!

Another rule for healthy substitution: Up to ½ cup sugar or less can be replaced by *an artificial sweetener that can withstand the heat of baking*, like pourable Sugar Twin or Sprinkle Sweet. If it requires more than ½ cup sugar, cut the amount needed by 75 percent and use ½ cup sugar substitute and sugar for the rest. Other options: reduce the butter and sugar by 25 percent and see if the finished product still satisfies you in taste and appearance. Or, make the cookies just like Grandma did, realizing they are part of your family's holiday tradition. Enjoy a *moderate* serving of a couple of cookies once or twice during the season, and just forget about them the rest of the year.

Did you know that you can replace the fat in many quick breads, muffins, and shortcakes with **fat-free mayonnaise** or **fat-free sour cream?** This can work if the original recipe doesn't call for a lot of fat *and* sugar. If the recipe is truly fat and sugar dependent, such as traditional sugar cookies, cupcakes, or pastries, it won't work. Those recipes require the large amounts of sugar and fat to make love in the dark of the oven to produce a tender finished product. But if you have a favorite quick bread that doesn't call for a lot of sugar or fat, why don't you give one of these substitutes a try?

If you enjoy beverage mixes like those from Alba, here are my Healthy Exchanges versions:

> For **chocolate-flavored,** use ⅓ cup nonfat dry milk powder and 2 tablespoons Nestlé Sugar-Free Chocolate Flavored Quik. Mix well and use as usual. Or, use ⅓ cup nonfat dry milk powder, 1 teaspoon unsweetened cocoa, and sugar substitute to equal 3 tablespoons sugar. Mix well and use as usual.
>
> For **vanilla-flavored,** use ⅓ cup nonfat dry milk powder, sugar substitute to equal 2 tablespoons sugar, and add 1 teaspoon vanilla extract when adding liquid.
>
> For **strawberry-flavored,** use ⅓ cup nonfat dry milk powder, sugar substitute to equal 2 tablespoons sugar, and add 1 teaspoon strawberry extract and 3–4 drops red food coloring when adding liquid.

Each of these makes one packet of drink mix. If you need to double the recipe, double everything but the extract. Use 1½ teaspoons of extract or it will be too strong. Use 1 cup cold water with one recipe mix to make a glass of flavored milk. If you want to make a shake, combine the mix, water, and 3–4 ice cubes in your blender, then process on BLEND till smooth.

A handy tip when making **healthy punch** for a party: prepare a few extra cups of your chosen drink, freeze it in cubes in a couple of ice trays, then keep your punch from "watering down" by cooling it with punch cubes instead.

What should you do if you can't find the product listed in a Healthy Exchanges recipe? You can substitute in some cases—use Lemon JELL-O if you can't find Hawaiian Pineapple, for example. But if you're determined to track down the product you need, and your own store manager hasn't been able to order it for you, why not use one of the new online grocers and order exactly what you need, no matter where you live. Try **http://www.netgrocer.com.**

Not all low-fat cooking products are interchangeable, as one of my readers recently discovered when she tried to cook pancakes on her griddle using I Can't Believe It's Not Butter! spray—

and they stuck! This butter-flavored spray is wonderful for a quick squirt on air-popped popcorn or corn on the cob, and it's great for topping your pancakes once they're cooked. In fact, my taste buds have to check twice because it tastes so much like real butter! (And this is high praise from someone who once thought butter was the most perfect food ever created.)

But I Can't Believe It's Not Butter! doesn't work well for sautéing or browning. After trying to fry an egg with it and cooking up a disaster, I knew this product had its limitations. So I decided to continue using Pam or Weight Watchers butter-flavored cooking spray whenever I'm browning anything in a skillet or on a griddle.

Many of my readers have reported difficulty finding a product I use in many recipes: JELL-O cook-and-serve puddings. I have three suggestions for those of you with this problem:

1. **Work with your grocery store manager to get this product into your store**, and then make sure you and everyone you know buys it by the bagful! Products that sell well are reordered and kept in stock, especially with today's computerized cash registers that record what's purchased. You may also want to write or call Kraft General Foods and ask for their help. They can be reached at (800) 431-1001 weekdays from 9 A.M. to 4 P.M. (EST).

2. **You can prepare the recipe that calls for cook-and-serve pudding by using instant pudding of the same flavor.** Yes, that's right, you **can** cook with the instant when making my recipes. The finished product won't be quite as wonderful, but still at least a 3 on a 4-star scale. You can never do the opposite—never use cook-and-serve in a recipe that calls for instant! One time at a cooking demonstration, I could not understand why my Blueberry Mountain Cheesecake never did set up. Then I spotted the box in the trash and noticed I'd picked the wrong type of pudding mix. Be careful—the boxes are both blue, but the instant has pudding on a silver spoon, and the cook-and-serve has a stream of milk running down the front into a bowl with a wooden spoon.

3. **You can make JO's Sugar-Free Vanilla Cook-and-Serve Pudding Mix instead of using JELL-O's.** Here's my

recipe: 2 tablespoons cornstarch, ½ cup pourable Sugar Twin or Sprinkle Sweet, ⅔ cup Carnation Nonfat Dry Milk Powder, 1½ cups water, 2 teaspoons vanilla extract, and 4 to 5 drops yellow food coloring. Combine all this in a medium saucepan and cook over medium heat, stirring constantly, until the mixture comes to a full boil and thickens. This is for basic cooked sugar-free vanilla pudding. For a chocolate version, the recipe is 2 tablespoons cornstarch, ¼ cup pourable Sugar Twin or Sprinkle Sweet, 2 tablespoons Nestlé's Sugar-Free Chocolate Flavored Quik, 1½ cups water, and 1 teaspoon vanilla extract. Follow the same cooking instructions as for the vanilla.

If you're preparing this as part of a recipe that also calls for adding a package of gelatin, just stir that into the mix.

Adapting a favorite family cake recipe? Here's something to try: Replace an egg and oil in the original with ⅓ cup plain fat-free yogurt and ¼ cup fat-free mayonnaise. Blend these two ingredients with your liquids in a separate bowl, then add the yogurt mixture to the flour mixture and mix gently just to combine. (You don't want to overmix or you'll release the gluten in the batter and end up with a tough batter.)

Want a tasty coffee creamer without all the fat? You could use Carnation's Fat Free Coffee-mate, which is 10 calories per teaspoon, but if you drink several cups a day with several teaspoons each, that adds up quickly to nearly 100 calories a day! Why not try my version? It's not quite as creamy, but it is good. Simply combine ⅓ cup Carnation Nonfat Dry Milk Powder and ¼ cup pourable Sugar Twin. Cover and store in your cupboard or refrigerator. At 3 calories per teaspoon, you can enjoy three teaspoons for less than the calories of one teaspoon of the purchased variety.

Some Helpful Hints

Sugar-free puddings and gelatins are important to many of my recipes, but if you prefer to avoid sugar substitutes, you could still prepare the recipes with regular puddings or gelatins. The calories would be higher, but you would still be cooking low-fat.

When a recipe calls for **chopped nuts** (and you only have whole ones), who wants to dirty the food processor just for a couple of tablespoonsful? You could try to chop them using your cutting board, but be prepared for bits and pieces to fly all over the kitchen. I use "Grandma's food processor." I take the biggest nuts I can find, put them in a small glass bowl, and chop them into chunks just the right size using a metal biscuit cutter.

A quick hint about **reduced-fat peanut butter:** Don't store it in the refrigerator. Because the fat has been reduced, it won't spread as easily when it's cold. Keep it in your cupboard and a little will spread a lot further.

Crushing **graham crackers** for topping? A self-seal sandwich bag works great!

If you have a **leftover muffin** and are looking for something a little different for breakfast, you can make a "**breakfast sundae.**" Crumble the muffin into a cereal bowl. Sprinkle a serving of fresh fruit over it and top with a couple of tablespoons of plain fat-free yogurt sweetened with sugar substitute and your choice of extract. The thought of it just might make you jump out of bed with a smile on your face. (Speaking of muffins, did you know that if you fill the unused muffin wells with water when baking muffins, you help ensure more even baking and protect the muffin pan at the same time?) Another muffin hint: Lightly spray the inside of paper baking cups with butter-flavored cooking spray before spooning the muffin batter into them. Then you won't end up with paper clinging to your fresh-baked muffins.

The secret of making **good meringues** without sugar is to use 1 tablespoon of Sprinkle Sweet or pourable Sugar Twin for every egg white, and a small amount of extract. Use ½ to 1 teaspoon for the batch. Almond, vanilla, and coconut are all good choices. Use the same amount of cream of tartar you usually do. Bake the meringue in the same old way. Even if you can't eat sugar, you can enjoy a healthy meringue pie when it's prepared the *Healthy Exchanges Way*. (Remember that egg whites whip up best at room temperature.)

Try **storing your Bisquick Reduced Fat Baking Mix** in the freezer. It won't freeze, and it *will* stay fresh much longer. (It works for coffee, doesn't it?)

If you've ever wondered about **changing ingredients** in one of my recipes, the answer is that some things can be changed to suit your family's tastes, but others should not be tampered with. **Don't change** the amount of flour, bread crumbs, reduced-fat baking mix, baking soda, baking powder, liquid, or dry milk powder. And if I include a small amount of salt, it's necessary for the recipe to turn out correctly. **What you can change:** an extract flavor (if you don't like coconut, choose vanilla or almond instead); a spreadable fruit flavor; the type of fruit in a pie filling (but be careful about substituting fresh for frozen and vice versa—sometimes it works but it may not); the flavor of pudding or gelatin. As long as package sizes and amounts are the same, go for it. It will never hurt my feelings if you change a recipe, so please your family—don't worry about me!

Because I always say that "good enough" isn't good enough for me anymore, here's a way to make your cup of **fat-free and sugar-free hot cocoa** more special. After combining the hot chocolate mix and hot water, stir in ½ teaspoon vanilla extract and a light sprinkle of cinnamon. If you really want to feel decadent, add a tablespoon of Cool Whip Lite. Isn't life grand?

If you must limit your sugar intake, but you love the idea of sprinkling **powdered sugar** on dessert crepes or burritos, here's a pretty good substitute: Place 1 cup Sprinkle Sweet or pourable Sugar Twin and 1 teaspoon cornstarch in a blender container, then cover and process on HIGH until the mixture resembles powdered sugar in texture, about 45 to 60 seconds. Store in an airtight container and use whenever you want a dusting of "powdered sugar" on any dessert.

Want my "almost instant" pies to set up even more quickly? Do as one of my readers does: freeze your Keebler piecrusts. Then, when you stir up one of my pies and pour the filling into the frozen crust, it sets up within seconds.

Some of my "island-inspired" recipes call for **rum or brandy extracts**, which provide the "essence" of liquor without the real thing. I'm a teetotaler by choice, so I choose not to include real liquor in any of my recipes. They're cheaper than liquor and you won't feel the need to shoo your kids away from the goodies. If you prefer not to use liquor extracts in your cooking, you can always substitute vanilla extract.

Some Healthy Cooking Challenges and How I Solved 'Em

When you stir up one of my pie fillings, do you ever have a problem with **lumps?** Here's an easy solution for all of you "careful" cooks out there. Lumps occur when the pudding starts to set up before you can get the dry milk powder incorporated into the mixture. I always advise you to dump, pour, and stir fast with that wire whisk, letting no more than 30 seconds elapse from beginning to end.

But if you are still having problems, you can always combine the dry milk powder and the water in a separate bowl before adding the pudding mix and whisking quickly. Why don't I suggest this right from the beginning? Because that would mean an extra dish to wash every time—and you know I hate to wash dishes!

With a little practice and a light touch, you should soon get the hang of my original method. But now you've got an alternative way to lose those lumps!

I love the chemistry of foods and so I've gotten great pleasure from analyzing what makes fat-free products tick. By dissecting these "miracle" products, I've learned how to make them work best. They require different handling than the high-fat products we're used to, but if treated properly, these slimmed-down versions can produce delicious results!

Fat-free sour cream: This product is wonderful on a hot baked potato, but have you noticed that it tends to be much gummier than regular sour cream? If you want to use it in a stroganoff dish or baked product, you must stir a tablespoon or two of skim milk into the fat-free sour cream before adding it to other ingredients.

Cool Whip Free: When the fat went out of the formula, air was stirred in to fill the void. So, if you stir it too vigorously, you release the air and *decrease* the volume. Handle it with kid gloves— gently. Since the manufacturer forgot to ask for my input, I'll share with you how to make it taste almost the same as it used to. Let the container thaw in the refrigerator, then ever so gently stir in 1 teaspoon vanilla extract. Now, put the lid back on and enjoy it a tablespoon at a time, the same way you did Cool Whip Lite.

Fat-free cream cheese: When the fat was removed from this product, water replaced it. So don't ever use an electric mixer on the fat-free version, or you risk releasing the water and having your finished product look more like dip than cheesecake! Stirring it gently with a sturdy spoon in a glass bowl with a handle will soften it just as much as it needs to be. And don't be alarmed if the cream cheese gets caught in your wire whisk when you start combining the pudding mix and other ingredients. Just keep knocking it back down into the bowl by hitting the whisk against the rim of the bowl, and as you continue blending, it will soften even more and drop off the whisk. When it's time to pour the filling into your crust, your whisk shouldn't have anything much clinging to it.

Reduced-fat margarine: Again, the fat was replaced by water. If you try to use the reduced-fat kind in your cookie recipe spoon for spoon, you will end up with a cake-like cookie instead of the crisp kind most of us enjoy. You have to take into consideration that some water will be released as the product bakes. Use less liquid than the recipe calls for (when re-creating family recipes *only*—I've figured this into Healthy Exchanges recipes). And never, never, never use fat-*free* margarine and expect anyone to ask for seconds!

Homemade or Store-Bought?

I've been asked which is better for you: homemade from scratch, or purchased foods. My answer is *both!* Each has a place in a healthy lifestyle, and what that place is has everything to do with you.

Take **piecrusts**, for instance. If you love spending your spare time in the kitchen preparing foods, and you're using low-fat, low-sugar, and reasonably low-sodium ingredients, go for it! But if, like so many people, your time is limited and you've learned to read labels, you could be better off using purchased foods.

I know that when I prepare a pie (and I experiment with a couple of pies each week, because this is Cliff's favorite dessert), I use a purchased crust. Why? Mainly because I can't make a good-tasting piecrust that is lower in fat than the brands I use. Also, purchased piecrusts fit my rule of "If it takes longer to fix than to eat, forget it!"

I've checked the nutrient information for the purchased

piecrusts against recipes for traditional and "diet" piecrusts, using my computer software program. The purchased crust calculated lower in both fat and calories! I have tried some low-fat and low-sugar recipes, but they just didn't spark my taste buds, or were so complicated you needed an engineering degree just to get the crust in the pie plate.

I'm very happy with the purchased piecrusts in my recipes, because the finished product rarely, if ever, has more than 30 percent of total calories coming from fats. I also believe that we have to prepare foods our families and friends will eat with us on a regular basis and not feel deprived, or we've wasted time, energy, and money.

I could use a purchased "lite" **pie filling**, but instead I make my own. Here I can save both fat and sugar, and still make the filling almost as fast as opening a can. The bottom line: Know what you have to spend when it comes to both time and fat/sugar calories, then make the best decision you can for you and your family. And don't go without an occasional piece of pie because you think it isn't *necessary*. A delicious pie prepared in a healthy way is one of the simple pleasures of life. It's a little thing, but it can make all the difference between just getting by with the bare minimum and living a full and healthy lifestyle.

I'm sure you'll add to this list of cooking tips as you begin preparing Healthy Exchanges recipes and discover how easy it can be to adapt your own favorite recipes using these ideas and your own common sense.

A Peek into
My Pantry and My
Favorite Brands

Everyone asks me what foods I keep on hand and what brands I use. There are lots of good products on the grocery shelves today—many more than we dreamed about even a year or two ago. And I can't wait to see what's out there twelve months from now. The following are my staples and, where appropriate, my favorites *at this time*. I feel these products are healthier, tastier, easy to get—and deliver the most flavor for the least amount of fat, sugar, or calories. If you find others you like as well *or better,* please use them. This is only a guide to make your grocery shopping and cooking easier. (You'll note that I've supplied you with my entire current list of favorites, even though some products are not used in any of my desserts. I hope this makes your shopping easier.)

Fat-free plain yogurt (*Yoplait or Dannon*)
Nonfat dry milk powder (*Carnation*)
Evaporated skim milk (*Carnation*)
Skim milk
Fat-free cottage cheese
Fat-free cream cheese (*Philadelphia*)
Fat-free mayonnaise (*Kraft*)
Fat-free salad dressings (*Kraft*)
Fat-free sour cream (*Land O Lakes*)
Reduced-calorie margarine (*Weight Watchers, Promise, or Smart Beat*)

Cooking spray
  Olive oil–flavored and regular (*Pam*)
  Butter-flavored for sautéing (*Pam or Weight Watchers*)
  Butter-flavored for spritzing *after* cooking (*I Can't Believe It's Not Butter!*)
Vegetable oil (*Puritan Canola Oil*)
Reduced-calorie whipped topping (*Cool Whip Lite or Cool Whip Free*)
Sugar substitute
  if no heating is involved (*Equal*)
  if heating is required
    white (*pourable Sugar Twin or Sprinkle Sweet*)
    brown (*Brown Sugar Twin*)
Sugar-free gelatin and pudding mixes (*JELL-O*)
Baking mix (*Bisquick Reduced Fat*)
Pancake mix (*Aunt Jemima Reduced-Calorie*)
Reduced-calorie pancake syrup (*Cary's Sugar Free*)
Parmesan cheese (*Kraft fat-free*)
Reduced-fat cheese (*Kraft 2% Reduced Fat*)
Shredded frozen potatoes (*Mr. Dell's*)
Spreadable fruit spread (*Smucker's, Welch's, or Knott's Berry Farm*)
Peanut butter (*Peter Pan reduced-fat, Jif reduced-fat, or Skippy reduced-fat*)
Chicken broth (*Healthy Request*)
Beef broth (*Swanson*)
Tomato sauce (*Hunt's—plain, Italian, or chili*)
Canned soups (*Healthy Request*)
Tomato juice (*Campbell's Reduced-Sodium*)
Ketchup (*Heinz Light Harvest or Healthy Choice*)
Purchased piecrust
  unbaked (*Pillsbury—from dairy case*)
  graham cracker, butter-flavored, or chocolate-flavored (*Keebler*)
Crescent rolls (*Pillsbury Reduced Fat*)
Pastrami and corned beef (*Carl Buddig Lean*)
Luncheon meats (*Healthy Choice or Oscar Mayer*)
Ham (*Dubuque 97% fat-free and reduced-sodium or Healthy Choice*)

Frankfurters and kielbasa sausage (*Healthy Choice*)
Canned white chicken, packed in water (*Swanson*)
Canned tuna, packed in water (*Starkist or Chicken of the Sea*)
90-95 percent lean ground turkey and beef
Soda crackers (*Nabisco Fat-Free*)
Reduced-calorie bread—40 calories per slice or less
Hamburger buns—80 calories each (*Less*)
Rice—instant, regular, brown, and wild
Instant potato flakes (*Betty Crocker Potato Buds*)
Noodles, spaghetti, and macaroni
Salsa (*Chi-Chi's Mild Chunky*)
Pickle relish—dill, sweet, and hot dog
Mustard—Dijon, prepared, and spicy
Unsweetened apple juice
Unsweetened applesauce
Fruit—fresh, frozen (no sugar added), or canned in juice
Vegetables—fresh, frozen, or canned
Spices—JO's Spices
Lemon and lime juice (in small plastic fruit-shaped bottles
    found in the produce section)
Instant fruit beverage mixes (*Crystal Light*)
Dry dairy beverage mixes (*Nestlé Quik*)
Ice cream (*Wells' Blue Bunny sugar- and fat-free*)

The items on my shopping list are everyday foods found in just about any grocery store in America. But all are as low in fat, sugar, calories, and sodium as I can find—and still taste good! I can make any recipe in my cookbooks and newsletters as long as I have my cupboards and refrigerator stocked with these items. Whenever I use the last of any one item, I just make sure I pick up another supply the next time I'm at the store.

If your grocer does not stock these items, why not ask if they can be ordered on a trial basis? If the store agrees to do so, be sure to tell your friends to stop by, so that sales are good enough to warrant restocking the new products. Competition for shelf space is fierce, so only products that sell well stay around.

Shopping
the Healthy
Exchanges Way

Sometimes, as part of a cooking demonstration, I take the group on a field trip to the nearest supermarket. There's no better place to share my discoveries about which healthy products taste best, which are best for you, and which healthy products don't deliver enough taste to include in my recipes.

While I'd certainly enjoy accompanying you to your neighborhood store, we'll have to settle for a field trip *on paper*. I've tasted and tried just about every fat- and sugar-free product on the market, but so many new ones keep coming all the time, you're going to have to learn to play detective on your own. I've turned label reading into an art, but often the label doesn't tell me everything I need to know.

Sometimes you'll find, as I have, that the product with *no* fat doesn't provide the taste satisfaction you require; other times, a no-fat or low-fat product just doesn't cook up the same way as the original product. And some foods, including even the leanest meats, can't eliminate *all* the fat. That's okay, though—a healthy diet should include anywhere from 15 to 25 percent of total calories from fat on any given day.

Take my word for it—your supermarket is filled with lots of delicious foods that can and should be part of your healthy diet for life. Come, join me as we check it out on the way to the checkout!

Before I buy anything at the store, I read the label carefully: I check the total fat plus the saturated fat; I look to see how many calories are in a realistic serving, and I say to myself, Would I eat that much—or would I eat more? I look at the sodium and I look at the total carbohydrates. I like to check those ingredients because I'm cooking for diabetics and heart patients too. And I check the total calories from fat.

Remember that 1 fat gram equals 9 calories, while 1 protein or 1 carbohydrate gram equals 4 calories.

A wonderful new product is I Can't Believe It's Not Butter! spray, with zero calories and zero grams of fat in five squirts. It's great for your air-popped popcorn. As for **light margarine spread**, beware—most of the fat-free brands don't melt on toast, and they don't taste very good either, so I just leave them on the shelf. For the few times I do use a light margarine I tend to buy Smart Beat Ultra, Promise Ultra, or Weight Watchers Light Ultra. The number-one ingredient in them is water. I occasionally use the light margarine in cooking, but I don't really put margarine on my toast anymore. I use apple butter or make a spread with fat-free cream cheese mixed with a little spreadable fruit instead.

So far, Pillsbury hasn't released a reduced-fat **crescent roll**, so you'll only get one crescent roll per serving from me. I usually make eight of the rolls serve twelve by using them for a crust. The house brands may be lower in fat but they're usually not as good flavor-wise—and they don't quite cover the pan when you use them to make a crust. If you're going to use crescent rolls with lots of other stuff on top, then a house brand might be fine.

The Pillsbury French Loaf makes a wonderful **pizza crust** and fills a giant jelly-roll pan. One-fifth of this package "costs" you only 1 gram of fat (and I don't even let you have that much!). Once you use this for your pizza crust, you will never go back to anything else instead. I use it to make calzones too.

I use only Philadelphia fat-free **cream cheese** because it has the best consistency. I've tried other brands, but I wasn't happy with them. Healthy Choice makes lots of great products, but their cream cheese just doesn't work as well with my recipes.

Let's move to the **cheese** aisle. My preferred brand is Kraft 2% Reduced Fat Shredded Cheeses. I will not use the fat-free versions because *they don't melt*. I would gladly give up sugar and fat, but I will not give up flavor. This is a happy compromise. I use the reduced-fat version, I use less, and I use it where your eyes "eat" it, on top of the recipe. So you walk away satisfied and with a finished product that's very low in fat. If you want to make grilled cheese sandwiches for your kids, use the Kraft reduced-fat cheese slices, and they'll taste exactly like the ones they're used to. The fat-free will not.

Dubuque's Extra-Lean Reduced-Sodium **ham** tastes wonderful, reduces the sodium as well as the fat, and gives you a larger serving. Don't be fooled by products called turkey ham; they may *not* be lower in fat than a very lean pork product. Here's one label as an example: I checked a brand of turkey ham called Genoa. It gives you a 2-ounce serving for 70 calories and 3½ grams of fat. The Dubuque extra-lean ham, made from pork, gives you a 3-ounce serving for 90 calories, but only 2½ grams of fat. *You get more food and less fat.*

Frozen dinners can be expensive and high in sodium, but it's smart to have two or three in the freezer as a backup when your best-laid plans go awry and you need to grab something on the run. It's not a good idea to rely on them too much—what if you can't get to the store to get them, or you're short on cash? The sodium can be high on some of them because they often replace the fat with salt, so be sure to read the labels. Also ask yourself if the serving is enough to satisfy you; for many of us, it's not.

Egg substitute is expensive, and probably not necessary unless you're cooking for someone who has to worry about every bit of cholesterol in his or her diet. If you occasionally have a fried egg or an omelet, *use the real egg.* For cooking, you can usually substitute two egg whites for one whole egg. Most of the time it won't make any difference, but check your recipe carefully.

Healthy frozen desserts are hard to find except for the Weight Watchers brands. I've always felt that their portions are so small, and for their size still pretty high in fat and sugar. (This is one of the reasons I think I'll be successful marketing my frozen desserts someday. After Cliff tasted one of my earliest healthy pies—and licked the plate clean—he remarked that if I ever opened a restaurant, people would keep coming back for my desserts alone!) Keep an eye out for fat-free or very low-fat frozen yogurt or sorbet products. Even Häagen-Dazs, which makes some of the highest-fat-content ice cream, now has a fat-free fruit sorbet pop out that's pretty good. I'm sure there will be more before too long.

You have to be realistic: What are you willing to do, and what are you *not* willing to do? Let's take **bread**, for example. Some people just have to have the real thing—rye bread with caraway seeds or a whole-wheat version with bits of bran in it. I prefer to use reduced-calorie bread because I like a *real sandwich*. This way, I can have two slices of bread and it counts as only one Bread/Starch exchange.

How I Shop for Myself

I always keep my kitchen stocked with my basic staples; that way, I can go to the cupboard and create new recipes any time I'm inspired. I hope you will take the time (and allot the money) to stock your cupboards with items from the staples list, so you can enjoy developing your own healthy versions of family favorites without making extra trips to the market.

I'm always on the lookout for new products sitting on the grocery shelf. When I spot something I haven't seen before, I'll usually grab it, glance at the front, then turn it around and read the label carefully. I call it looking at the "promises" (the "come-on" on the front of the package) and then at the "warranty" (the ingredients list and the label on the back).

If it looks as good on the back as it does on the front, I'll say okay and either create a recipe on the spot or take it home for when I do think of something to do with it. Picking up a new product is just about the only time I buy something not on my list.

The items on my shopping list are normal, everyday foods, but as low-fat and low-sugar (*while still tasting good*) as I can find. I can make any recipe in this book as long as these staples are on my shelves. After using these products for a couple of weeks, you will find it becomes routine to have them on hand. And I promise you, I really don't spend any more at the store now than I did a few years ago when I told myself I couldn't afford some of these items. Back then, of course, plenty of unhealthy, high-priced snacks I really didn't need somehow made the magic leap from the grocery shelves into my cart. Who was I kidding?

Yes, you often have to pay a little more for fat-free or low-fat products, including meats. But since I frequently use a half pound of meat to serve four to six people, your cost per serving will be much lower.

Try adding up what you were spending before on chips and cookies, premium-brand ice cream, and fatty cuts of meat, and you'll soon see that we've *streamlined* your shopping cart, and taken the weight off your pocketbook as well as your hips!

Remember, your good health is *your* business—but it's big business too. Write to the manufacturers of products you and your family enjoy but feel are just too high in fat, sugar, or sodium to be part of your new healthy lifestyle. Companies are spending millions of dollars to respond to consumers' concerns about food products, and I bet that in the next few years, you'll discover fat-free and low-fat versions of nearly every product piled high on your supermarket shelves!

The Healthy Exchanges Kitchen

You might be surprised to discover I still don't have a massive test kitchen stocked with every modern appliance and handy gadget ever made. The tiny galley kitchen where I first launched Healthy Exchanges has room for only one person at a time, but it never stopped me from feeling the sky's the limit when it comes to seeking out great healthy taste!

Because storage is at such a premium in my kitchen, I don't waste space with equipment I don't really need. Here's a list of what I consider worth having. If you notice serious gaps in your equipment, you can probably find most of what you need at a local discount store or garage sale. If your kitchen is equipped with more sophisticated appliances, don't feel guilty about using them. Enjoy every appliance you can find room for or that you can afford. Just be assured that healthy, quick, and delicious food can be prepared with the "basics."

A Healthy Exchanges Kitchen Equipment List

Good-quality nonstick skillets (medium, large)
Good-quality saucepans (small, medium, large)
Glass mixing bowls (small, medium, large)

Glass measures (1-cup, 2-cup, 4-cup, 8-cup)
Sharp knives (paring, chef, butcher)
Rubber spatulas
Wire whisks   4-inch round custard dishes
Measuring spoons   Glass pie plates
Measuring cups   8-by-8-inch glass baking dishes
Large mixing spoons   Cake pans (9-by-9-inch, 9-by-13-inch)
Egg separator   10¾-by-7-by-1½-inch biscuit pan
Covered jar   Cookie sheets (good nonstick ones)
Vegetable parer   Jelly-roll pan
Grater   Muffin tins
Potato masher   5-by-9-inch bread pan
Electric mixer   Plastic colander
Electric blender   Cutting board
Electric skillet   Pie wedge server
Cooking timer   Square-shaped server
Slow cooker   Can opener (I prefer manual)
Air popper for popcorn   Rolling pin
Kitchen scales (unless you *always* use my recipes)
Wire racks for cooling baked goods
Electric toaster oven (to conserve energy for those times when only
one item is being baked or for a recipe that requires a short baking
time)

How to Read a Healthy Exchanges Recipe

The Healthy Exchanges Nutritional Analysis

Before using these recipes, you may wish to consult your physician or health-care provider to be sure they are appropriate for you. The information in this book is not intended to take the place of any medical advice. It reflects my experiences, studies, research, and opinions regarding healthy eating.

Each recipe includes nutritional information calculated in three ways:

> Healthy Exchanges Weight Loss Choices™ or Exchanges
> Calories; Fat, Protein, Carbohydrates, and Fiber in grams;
> Sodium and Calcium in milligrams
> Diabetic exchanges

In every Healthy Exchanges recipe, the diabetic exchanges have been calculated by a registered dietitian. All the other calculations were done by computer, using the Food Processor II software. When the ingredient listing gives more than one choice, the first ingredient listed is the one used in the recipe analysis. Due to inevitable variations in the ingredients you choose to use, the nutritional values should be considered approximate.

The annotation "(limited)" following Protein counts in some recipes indicates that consumption of whole eggs should be limited to four per week.

Please note the following symbols:

☆ This star means read the recipe's directions carefully for special instructions about **division** of ingredients.

❋ This symbol indicates **FREEZES WELL.**

A Few
Cooking Terms to
Ease the Way

Everyone can learn to cook the *Healthy Exchanges Way*. It's simple, it's quick, and the results are delicious! If you've tended to avoid the kitchen because you find recipe instructions confusing or complicated, I hope I can help you feel more confident. I'm not offering a full cooking course here, just some terms I use often that I know you'll want to understand.

Bake: To cook food in the oven; sometimes called roasting

Beat: To mix very fast with a spoon, wire whisk, or electric mixer

Blend: To mix two or more ingredients together thoroughly so that the mixture is smooth

Boil: To cook in liquid until bubbles form

Brown: To cook at low to medium-low heat until ingredients turn brown

Chop: To cut food into small pieces with a knife, blender, or food processor

Combine: To mix ingredients together with a spoon

Cool: To let stand at room temperature until food is no longer hot to the touch

Dice: To chop into small, even-sized pieces

Drain: To pour off liquid; sometimes you will need to reserve the liquid to use in the recipe, so please read carefully

Drizzle: To sprinkle drops of liquid (for example, chocolate syrup) lightly over the top of food

Fold in: To combine delicate ingredients with other foods by using a gentle, circular motion (for example, adding Cool Whip Lite to an already stirred-up bowl of pudding)

Preheat: To heat your oven to the desired temperature, usually about 10 minutes before you put your food in to bake

Sauté: To cook in a skillet or frying pan until the food is soft

Simmer: To cook in a small amount of liquid over low heat; this lets the flavors blend without too much liquid evaporating

Whisk: To beat with a wire whisk until mixture is well mixed; don't worry about finesse here, just use some elbow grease!

How to Measure

I try to make it as easy as possible by providing more than one measurement for many ingredients in my recipes—both the weight in ounces and the amount measured by a measuring cup, for example. Just remember:

- You measure **solids** (flour, Cool Whip Lite, yogurt, nonfat dry milk powder) in your set of separate measuring cups (¼, ⅓, ½, 1 cup)

- You measure **liquids** (Diet Mountain Dew, water, juice) in the clear glass or plastic measuring cups that measure ounces, cups, and pints. Set the cup on a level surface and pour the liquid into it, or you may get too much.

- You can use your measuring spoon set for liquids or solids. **Note:** Don't pour a liquid like an extract into a measuring spoon held over the bowl in case you overpour; instead, do it over the sink.

Here are a few handy equivalents:

3 teaspoons	equals	1 tablespoon
4 tablespoons	equals	¼ cup
5⅓ tablespoons	equals	⅓ cup
8 tablespoons	equals	½ cup
10⅔ tablespoons	equals	⅔ cup

12 tablespoons	equals	¾ cup
16 tablespoons	equals	1 cup
2 cups	equals	1 pint
4 cups	equals	1 quart
8 ounces liquid	equals	1 fluid cup

That's it. Now, ready, set, cook!

The Recipes

Vegetable Soups

Even if your grandma or mom never made soup from scratch, you probably grew up loving vegetable soup—the heartwarming, soothing kind from the can with the little veggie chunks and the alphabet letters that you could use to spell your name! In our house, soup was often the answer when the kids asked, "What's for lunch?" or "What's for supper?" Because we always had a garden, we had fresh vegetables we grew ourselves during most months of the year. Even during the worst of snowy winters, we had potatoes, carrots, beans, and turnips stored in the root cellar and pantry that could be magically transformed into a hearty and satisfying meal.

I think every family in Iowa must have at least a couple of recipes for corn soups that have been handed down from mother to daughter over the generations. When you grow up surrounded by cornfields, you can't help but experience the changing seasons while watching the corn grow: first, snow-covered fields that make you wonder if spring will ever come; then the soft mud of spring inviting the seed that will grow into stalks, beautifully green and amazingly tall by summer's end. Fall brings shorter days and colder nights, when a bowl of soup eaten before a roaring fire is a meal fit for a king.

My Healthy Exchanges vegetable soups still celebrate the bounty of the harvest, but they also use top-quality convenience foods that will deliver a truly luscious result in very little time. Whether your taste buds tingle at the thought of a rich tomato soup (Tomato Corn Soup), or you're dreaming of a luscious and creamy mushroom soup (Magic Cream of Mushroom Soup), or you just want a big bowl of cozy warmth that will feed your soul as well as your tummy (Hearty Borscht or French Cauliflower Soup), you'll find it in here!

Vegetable
Soups

Egg Flower Soup

Here's a delicate broth made especially pretty by the addition of five-spice powder and those pale yellow threads of egg. It's a light soup, a wonderful contrast to many of the heartier choices in this book, but a good one to have in your repertoire.

◐ Serves 4 (1¼ cups)

> 4 cups (two 16-ounce cans) Healthy Request Chicken Broth
> 1 cup frozen peas
> ½ cup (one 2.5-ounce jar) sliced mushrooms, drained
> ½ cup (3 ounces) finely diced cooked chicken breast
> 1 egg, beaten, or equivalent in egg substitute
> ½ teaspoon Oriental seasoning

In a large saucepan, combine chicken broth, peas, mushrooms, and chicken. Bring mixture to a boil. Lower heat, cover and simmer for 5 minutes. In a small bowl, combine egg and Oriental seasoning with a fork. Slowly pour egg mixture into hot soup in a thin stream, stirring very gently until egg is set. Serve at once.

HINT: If you don't have leftovers, purchase a chunk of cooked chicken breast from your local deli.

Each serving equals:

> HE: 1 Protein (¼ limited) • ½ Bread •
> ¼ Vegetable • 16 Optional Calories
> ___
> 102 Calories • 2 gm Fat • 14 gm Protein •
> 7 gm Carbohydrate • 596 mg Sodium •
> 21 mg Calcium • 2 gm Fiber
> ___
> DIABETIC: 1 Meat • ½ Starch

Vegetable Egg Drop Soup

This delicate and very low-calorie soup is inspired by the traditional egg drop soup served in Chinese restaurants everywhere. I've added a melange of vegetables to give it more "oomph"—enjoy!

◐ Serves 4 (1¼ cups)

> 4 cups (two 16-ounce cans) Healthy Request Chicken Broth
> 1¾ cups shredded cabbage
> ½ cup shredded carrots
> ½ cup finely chopped celery
> ¼ cup finely chopped onion
> 1 egg, beaten, or equivalent in egg substitute
> ¼ teaspoon lemon pepper

In a medium saucepan, combine chicken broth, cabbage, carrots, celery, and onion. Bring mixture to a boil, stirring occasionally. Lower heat, cover, and simmer for 15 minutes or until vegetables are just tender. In a small bowl, combine egg and lemon pepper with a fork. Slowly pour egg mixture into hot soup in a thin stream, stirring very gently until egg is set. Serve at once.

Each serving equals:

HE: 1½ Vegetable • ¼ Protein (limited) •
16 Optional Calories

---

53 Calories • 1 gm Fat • 5 gm Protein •
6 gm Carbohydrate • 519 mg Sodium •
32 mg Calcium • 1 gm Fiber

DIABETIC: 1 Vegetable • 1 Free Vegetable

Magic Cream of Mushroom Soup ❄

I often talk about whisking out the fat with my magic whisk, but in this case I definitely had some help! Here's a perfect example of the "abracadabra" you can create by stirring in some nonfat dry milk powder blended with just a bit of flour. Thick and creamy soup every time—it's gotta be magic!   ☺   Serves 4 (1 cup)

2½ cups finely chopped fresh mushrooms
½ cup finely chopped onion
2 cups (one 16-ounce can) Healthy Request Chicken Broth
¼ teaspoon dried minced garlic
⅛ teaspoon black pepper
1⅓ cups Carnation Nonfat Dry Milk Powder
3 tablespoons all-purpose flour
1 cup water
½ teaspoon dried basil

In an 8-cup glass measuring bowl, combine mushrooms, onion, chicken broth, garlic, and black pepper. Microwave on HIGH (100% power) for 6 minutes, stirring after 2 minutes. In a covered jar, combine dry milk powder, flour, water, and basil. Shake well to blend. Stir milk mixture into mushroom mixture. Continue microwaving on HIGH for 6 minutes, stirring after every 2 minutes.

Each serving equals:

HE: 1½ Vegetable • 1 Skim Milk •
¼ Bread • 8 Optional Calories

---

128 Calories • 0 gm Fat • 11 gm Protein •
21 gm Carbohydrate • 367 mg Sodium •
290 mg Calcium • 1 gm Fiber

DIABETIC: 1 Skim Milk • ½ Vegetable

Chunky Italian Tomato Soup

Tomato soup is famous for its smooth and luscious texture, but I thought adding some "chunks" of veggies and some tangy spice would lend a little sparkle to this beloved classic! (Maybe if we all wish really hard, they'll bring back those chunky tomato sauces I loved to cook with. . . .)   ❂   Serves 4 (1 cup)

½ cup finely chopped onion
1 cup (one 8-ounce can) Hunt's Tomato Sauce
1 (10¾-ounce) can Healthy Request Tomato Soup
1½ cups (one 12-fluid-ounce can) Carnation Evaporated Skim
    Milk
¾ cup water
½ cup (one 2.5-ounce jar) sliced mushrooms, drained
1 teaspoon Italian seasoning
⅛ teaspoon black pepper

In a large saucepan sprayed with olive oil–flavored cooking spray, sauté onion for 5 minutes or until tender. Stir in tomato sauce, tomato soup, evaporated skim milk, and water. Add mushrooms, Italian seasoning, and black pepper. Mix well to combine. Lower heat and simmer for 6 to 8 minutes or until mixture is heated through, stirring occasionally.

Each serving equals:

HE: 1¼ Vegetable • ¾ Skim Milk •
½ Slider • 5 Optional Calories

---

161 Calories • 1 gm Fat • 10 gm Protein •
28 gm Carbohydrate • 762 mg Sodium •
307 mg Calcium • 3 gm Fiber

DIABETIC: 1 Vegetable • ½ Starch/Carbohydrate

Grandma's Cream of Tomato Soup

Didn't it always seem as if she stirred and stirred and stirred it for hours, so that your grandma's creamy tomato soup was a little taste of heaven in a pretty bowl? Well, get out your favorite soup dishes, put this truly cozy soup on the menu, and just see if your family isn't convinced they're dining with the angels!

◔ Serves 4 (1 cup)

> 3 cups peeled and chopped fresh tomatoes
> ½ cup finely chopped celery
> ½ cup finely chopped onion
> ⅔ cup Carnation Nonfat Dry Milk Powder
> 3 tablespoons all-purpose flour
> 1¼ cups water
> 2 teaspoons pourable Sugar Twin
> 1½ teaspoons dried parsley flakes
> ⅛ teaspoon black pepper
> ¼ cup Land O Lakes no-fat sour cream

In a medium saucepan, combine tomatoes, celery, and onion. Cover and cook over medium-low heat for 10 to 12 minutes or until tomatoes are soft, stirring often. Place saucepan on a wire rack and let set for 10 minutes. Pour partially cooled tomato mixture into a blender container. Cover and process on BLEND for 45 seconds or until mixture is smooth. In a covered jar, combine dry milk powder, flour, and water. Shake well to blend. Pour milk mixture into a large saucepan sprayed with butter-flavored cooking spray. Cook over medium heat for 6 to 8 minutes or until mixture thickens, stirring constantly. Gradually stir tomato mixture into milk mixture. Add Sugar Twin, parsley flakes, and black pepper. Mix well to combine. Lower heat and simmer for 6 to 8 minutes or until mixture is heated through, stirring often. When serving, top each bowl with 1 tablespoon sour cream.

Each serving equals:

HE: 2 Vegetable • ½ Skim Milk • ¼ Bread •
16 Optional Calories

---

112 Calories • 0 gm Fat • 7 gm Protein •
21 gm Carbohydrate • 108 mg Sodium •
174 mg Calcium • 2 gm Fiber

DIABETIC: 2 Vegetable • ½ Skim Milk

Bombay Fresh Tomato Soup

I just read that India is one of the hottest tourist destinations these days, but for most of us, a trip overseas isn't in the cards this year. Instead, why not serve up a culinary visit to that exotic country—and begin with this glorious celebration of the ripe tomato?

◐ Serves 6 (1 full cup)

1 cup finely chopped celery
½ cup chopped onion
1 cup shredded carrots
½ cup chopped green bell pepper
4 cups (two 16-ounce cans)
    Healthy Request Chicken
    Broth ☆
4 cups peeled and chopped
    fresh tomatoes

½ teaspoon curry powder
¼ teaspoon black pepper
1 tablespoon pourable
    Sugar Twin
1 cup fresh or frozen
    whole-kernel corn, thawed
3 tablespoons all-purpose flour

In a large saucepan sprayed with butter-flavored cooking spray, sauté celery, onion, carrots, and green pepper for 6 to 8 minutes or just until tender. Stir in 3½ cups chicken broth, tomatoes, curry powder, black pepper, and Sugar Twin. Bring mixture to a boil. Add corn. Mix well to combine. Lower heat and simmer for 20 minutes. In a small bowl, combine flour and remaining ½ cup chicken broth. Mix well using a wire whisk. Blend flour mixture into tomato mixture. Continue cooking for 5 minutes or until mixture is heated through and starts to thicken, stirring often.

HINT: Thaw corn by placing in a colander and rinsing under hot water for one minute.

Each serving equals:

HE: 2⅓ Vegetable • ½ Bread • 12 Optional Calories

92 Calories • 0 gm Fat • 4 gm Protein •
19 gm Carbohydrate • 357 mg Sodium •
25 mg Calcium • 3 gm Fiber

DIABETIC: 2 Vegetable • ½ Starch

Wild Rice and Tomato Soup ❄

You'll notice that I often use high-quality convenience foods in my recipes, but I always add special touches to deepen the flavors and improve the finished result! Here, my little extras produce a rich and creamy dish that's perfect for a dinner party.

○ Serves 4 (1¼ cups)

> ½ cup chopped onion
> 1 (10¾-ounce) can Healthy Request Tomato Soup
> 1½ cups (one 12-fluid-ounce can) Carnation Evaporated Skim
>   Milk
> 1 cup (one 8-ounce can) Hunt's Tomato Sauce
> ¾ cup water
> Scant 1 cup (3 ounces) uncooked instant long grain and wild rice
> 1 teaspoon dried parsley flakes
> ⅛ teaspoon black pepper

In a large saucepan sprayed with butter-flavored cooking spray, sauté onion for about 5 minutes. Stir in tomato soup, evaporated skim milk, tomato sauce, and water. Add uncooked rice, parsley flakes, and black pepper. Mix well to combine. Lower heat, cover, and simmer for about 10 minutes or until rice is tender, stirring occasionally.

Each serving equals:

HE: 1¼ Vegetable • 1 Bread • ¾ Skim Milk •
½ Slider • 5 Optional Calories

---

193 Calories • 1 gm Fat • 10 gm Protein •
36 gm Carbohydrate • 780 mg Sodium •
310 mg Calcium • 3 gm Fiber

DIABETIC: 1½ Starch • 1 Vegetable • 1 Skim Milk

Spinach Tomato Soup

Don't decide that the recipe instructions for this dish are nuts until you've tried them—you'll see how delectable sautéing fresh spinach leaves in fat-free dressing can be! This is a fantastic "leftovers" dish—just tear open a bag of spinach, use up some rice from an earlier meal, and stir in a few ingredients you keep handy all the time.

☻ Serves 4 (1 cup)

> 1 cup finely chopped fresh spinach leaves
> 2 tablespoons Kraft Fat Free Italian Dressing
> 1 (10¾-ounce) can Healthy Request Tomato Soup
> 1½ cups (one 12-fluid-ounce can) Carnation Evaporated Skim Milk
> 1 cup cold cooked rice
> ¼ cup (¾ ounce) grated Kraft fat-free Parmesan cheese

In a medium saucepan, sauté spinach in Italian dressing for about 5 minutes or just until tender. Add tomato soup and evaporated skim milk. Mix well to combine. Stir in rice. Continue cooking for about 5 minutes or until mixture is heated through, stirring often. When serving, sprinkle 1 tablespoon Parmesan cheese over top of each bowl.

HINT: ⅔ cup uncooked rice usually cooks to about 1 cup.

Each serving equals:

HE: ¾ Skim Milk • ½ Bread • ½ Vegetable • ¼ Protein • ½ Slider • 9 Optional Calories

---

181 Calories • 1 gm Fat • 10 gm Protein • 33 gm Carbohydrate • 509 mg Sodium • 303 mg Calcium • 2 gm Fiber

---

DIABETIC: 1 Starch • ½ Skim Milk

French Bean and Tomato Soup ❄

What an appetizing choice for a quick supper! This soup is ready in minutes, features flavors the whole family will love, and delivers lots of protein in every spoonful.   ☺   Serves 4 (1 cup)

1 (10¾-ounce) can Healthy Request Tomato Soup
1½ cups (one 12-fluid-ounce can) Carnation Evaporated Skim
    Milk
⅓ cup (1½ ounces) shredded Kraft reduced-fat Cheddar cheese
¼ teaspoon black pepper
2 cups (one 16-ounce can) French-style green beans, rinsed and
    drained
1 cup cooked noodles, rinsed and drained

In a large saucepan, combine tomato soup, evaporated skim milk, Cheddar cheese, and black pepper. Stir in green beans and noodles. Cook over medium heat for about 10 minutes or until mixture is heated through and cheese melts, stirring occasionally.

HINT: A scant 1 cup uncooked noodles usually cooks to about 1 cup.

Each serving equals:

HE: 1 Vegetable • ¾ Skim Milk • ½ Bread •
½ Protein • ½ Slider • 5 Optional Calories

211 Calories • 3 gm Fat • 13 gm Protein •
33 gm Carbohydrate • 433 mg Sodium •
378 mg Calcium • 2 gm Fiber

DIABETIC: 1 Vegetable • 1 Starch •
½ Skim Milk • ½ Meat

Tomato Corn Soup

Sometimes it's the spices that give a recipe real zing (they do here!), but often my readers tell me they don't know how much to add. Here's a bit of healthy cooking advice—start with the least you can measure, taste, then add a bit more. You can always add spices but once they're in the dish, an "overdose" is harder to handle!

☻ Serves 4 (1¼ cups)

> 1 (10¾-ounce) can Healthy Request Tomato Soup
> 1 cup (one 8-ounce can) Hunt's Tomato Sauce
> 1¾ cups water
> 2 tablespoons dried onion flakes
> 1 teaspoon dried parsley flakes
> 1 teaspoon dried basil
> 1½ cups frozen whole-kernel corn, thawed

In a medium saucepan, combine tomato soup, tomato sauce, and water. Stir in onion flakes, parsley flakes, and basil. Add corn. Mix well to combine. Cook over medium heat for about 10 minutes or until mixture is heated through, stirring occasionally.

HINT: Thaw corn by placing in a colander and rinsing under hot water for one minute.

Each serving equals:

HE: 1 Vegetable • ¾ Bread • ½ Slider • 5 Optional Calories

133 Calories • 1 gm Fat • 4 gm Protein • 27 gm Carbohydrate • 672 mg Sodium • 38 mg Calcium • 4 gm Fiber

DIABETIC: 1½ Starch • 1 Vegetable

Creamy Zucchini Tomato Rice Soup

Even if zucchini is not on your "favorite vegetable" list, you might just find this luscious veggie soup worthy of a bowl or two! That's the thing about soup—as it bubbles away on the stove, the ingredients tend to "shake hands" and share each other's best qualities.

❂ Serves 4 (1 cup)

> 1 cup chopped unpeeled zucchini
> 1 (10¾-ounce) can Healthy Request Tomato Soup
> 1½ cups (one 12-fluid-ounce can) Carnation Evaporated Skim
>   Milk
> ½ teaspoon dried basil leaves
> ¼ teaspoon dried minced garlic
> 1½ cups hot cooked rice
> ¼ cup (¾ ounce) grated Kraft fat-free Parmesan cheese

In a large saucepan sprayed with butter-flavored cooking spray, sauté zucchini for 5 minutes or just until tender. Add tomato soup, evaporated skim milk, basil, and garlic. Mix well to combine. Stir in rice. Lower heat and simmer for 6 to 8 minutes or until mixture is heated through, stirring occasionally. When serving, sprinkle 1 tablespoon Parmesan cheese over top of each bowl.

HINT: 1 cup uncooked rice usually cooks to about 1½ cups.

Each serving equals:

HE: ¾ Skim Milk • ¾ Bread • ½ Vegetable •
¼ Protein • ½ Slider • 5 Optional Calories

197 Calories • 1 gm Fat • 10 gm Protein •
37 gm Carbohydrate • 422 mg Sodium •
300 mg Calcium • 2 gm Fiber

DIABETIC: 1½ Starch • 1 Skim Milk

Tomato and Zucchini Stew with Parmesan Cheese Dumplings

We grow zucchini in our Healthy Exchanges garden, and yes, just as you may have experienced, we often find ourselves with more than we can use! That's when I set myself the challenge of coming up with fresh new ways to use this tasty green veggie. This one also incorporates luscious tomatoes picked ripe and red from your own plants—or from the nearest farmstand!

○ Serves 4 (1 cup stew and 2 dumplings)

2 tablespoons Kraft Fat Free Italian Dressing
½ cup chopped onion
3 cups peeled and chopped fresh tomatoes
1 teaspoon dried basil
2 tablespoons pourable Sugar Twin
¼ teaspoon black pepper
1½ cups chopped unpeeled zucchini
¾ cup Bisquick Reduced Fat Baking Mix
¼ cup (¾ ounce) grated Kraft fat-free Parmesan cheese
⅓ cup Carnation Nonfat Dry Milk Powder
½ cup water

Pour Italian dressing into a large skillet. Stir in onion. Cook over medium heat for 3 to 4 minutes, stirring often. Add tomatoes, basil, Sugar Twin, and black pepper. Mix well to combine. Lower heat, cover, and simmer for 10 minutes. Stir in zucchini. Re-cover and continue simmering for 10 minutes. In a small bowl, combine baking mix, Parmesan cheese, and dry milk powder. Add water. Mix well to combine. Drop batter by tablespoonful over tomato mixture to form 8 dumplings. Re-cover and continue simmering for 20 minutes or until dumplings are firm.

Each serving equals:

HE: 2½ Vegetable • 1 Bread • ¼ Skim Milk •
¼ Protein • 7 Optional Calories

170 Calories • 2 gm Fat • 6 gm Protein •
32 gm Carbohydrate • 464 mg Sodium •
114 mg Calcium • 3 gm Fiber

DIABETIC: 2 Vegetable • 1½ Starch/Carbohydrate

Tomato Soup with Bacon and Cheese Dumplings ❄

The fun of recipe creating is shaking up someone's expectations just a little from time to time! In this case, you've answered the question of "What's for dinner?" by saying, "Tomato soup," but you never let on about the little something extra you planned for a surprise. These dumplings are spectacular, and turn an everyday meal into a real feast.   ☻   Serves 4 (1 cup soup and 2 dumplings)

½ cup finely chopped onion
1 (10¾-ounce) can Healthy Request Tomato Soup
2 cups (one 16-ounce can) tomatoes, finely chopped and
    undrained
1½ cups (one 12-fluid-ounce can) Carnation Evaporated Skim
    Milk
1 teaspoon chili seasoning
1 teaspoon dried parsley flakes
¾ cup Bisquick Reduced Fat Baking Mix
3 tablespoons Hormel Bacon Bits
⅓ cup (1½ ounces) shredded Kraft reduced-fat Cheddar cheese
⅓ cup skim milk

In a large saucepan sprayed with butter-flavored cooking spray, sauté onion for 5 minutes or until tender. Stir in tomato soup, undrained tomatoes, evaporated skim milk, chili seasoning, and parsley flakes. Lower heat, cover, and simmer for 10 minutes, stirring occasionally. In a medium bowl, combine baking mix, bacon bits, Cheddar cheese, and skim milk. Let rest for 5 minutes. Drop batter by tablespoonful into hot soup to form 8 dumplings. Re-cover and continue simmering for 15 to 25 minutes or until dumplings are firm.

Each serving equals:

HE: 1¼ Vegetable • 1 Bread • ¾ Skim Milk •
½ Protein • ¾ Slider • 11 Optional Calories

265 Calories • 5 gm Fat • 17 gm Protein •
38 gm Carbohydrate • 860 mg Sodium •
409 mg Calcium • 2 gm Fiber

DIABETIC: 2 Starch • 1 Vegetable •
1 Skim Milk • ½ Meat

Tomato French Onion Soup

I love to take what is already delicious and see if I can make it just a little bit better. Or, as the French say, *meilleur!* In this case, I've introduced some tomato flavor into the standard beefy broth, and topped each bowl with delectable cheese and crisp toast. Put Paris on your culinary itinerary tonight, and after one spoonful, you're sure to say, "Ooh-la-la!"   ☻   Serves 4

4 cups chopped onion

1¾ cups (one 14½-ounce can) Swanson Beef Broth ☆

1 cup (one 8-ounce can) Hunt's Tomato Sauce

1¾ cups water

1 teaspoon dried basil

4 slices reduced-calorie French or Italian bread, toasted

4 (¾-ounce) slices Kraft reduced-fat Swiss cheese

Preheat oven to 350 degrees. In a large saucepan, combine onion and ¼ cup beef broth. Cook over medium heat for about 10 minutes or until onion is tender. Stir in tomato sauce, remaining 1½ cups beef broth, water, and basil. Bring mixture to a boil. Lower heat and simmer for 10 minutes. Evenly ladle soup into 4 oven-proof bowls. Top each with 1 slice toast and 1 slice Swiss cheese. Place bowls on a baking sheet. Bake for 10 minutes.

Each serving equals:

HE: 3 Vegetable • 1 Protein • ½ Bread • 9 Optional Calories

205 Calories • 5 gm Fat • 8 gm Protein • 32 gm Carbohydrate • 968 mg Sodium • 63 mg Calcium • 6 gm Fiber

DIABETIC: 3 Vegetable • 1 Meat • ½ Starch

Easy French Onion Soup

What a wonderful way to enjoy the sweet intensity of onion soup when you haven't got a lot of time but you want a lot of flavor. I think this would be extra-delicious prepared with sweet Vidalia onions, which are only available for a short time each year. They cost a little more, but the unique taste is worth it.

◐ Serves 4

3 cups sliced onion
1¾ cups (one 14½-ounce can) Swanson Beef Broth
2 cups water
1 teaspoon dried parsley flakes
⅛ teaspoon black pepper
2 slices reduced-calorie white bread, toasted and cubed
¼ cup (¾ ounce) grated Kraft fat-free Parmesan cheese

In a large saucepan sprayed with butter-flavored cooking spray, sauté onion for 8 to 10 minutes or until tender. Stir in beef broth, water, parsley flakes, and black pepper. Bring mixture to a boil. Lower heat and simmer for 6 to 8 minutes. For each serving, spoon about 1¼ cups soup in a bowl, stir ¼ of bread cubes into soup, and sprinkle 1 tablespoon Parmesan cheese over top. Serve at once.

Each serving equals:

HE: 1½ Vegetable • ¼ Bread • ¼ Protein •
8 Optional Calories

97 Calories • 1 gm Fat • 4 gm Protein •
18 gm Carbohydrate • 500 mg Sodium •
35 mg Calcium • 4 gm Fiber

DIABETIC: 1½ Vegetable • ½ Starch/Carbohydrate

Peasant's Swiss Onion Soup

Traditional onion soup prepared the classic French way uses a kind of cheese called Gruyère, but I think this recipe might give that one a run for its money! Try this with different kinds of onions for a varied result. Serves 4 (1½ cups)

3 cups finely chopped onion
1 cup water
3 cups skim milk
6 (¾-ounce) slices Kraft reduced-fat Swiss cheese, shredded
½ teaspoon paprika
½ teaspoon lemon pepper
4 slices reduced-calorie white bread, toasted and cubed
1 teaspoon dried parsley flakes

In a large saucepan sprayed with butter-flavored cooking spray, sauté onion for 8 to 10 minutes or just until tender. Stir in water and skim milk. Add Swiss cheese, paprika, and lemon pepper. Mix well to combine. Lower heat. Fold in bread cubes and parsley flakes. Cover and simmer for 20 minutes, stirring occasionally.

Each serving equals:

HE: 1½ Protein • 1½ Vegetable • ¾ Skim Milk • ½ Bread

260 Calories • 8 gm Fat • 17 gm Protein • 30 gm Carbohydrate • 708 mg Sodium • 269 mg Calcium • 5 gm Fiber

DIABETIC: 1 Meat • 1 Vegetable • 1 Skim Milk • ½ Starch

Chunky Gazpacho

This recipe takes seconds to prepare, but tastes better if you can give it a few hours in the fridge so all the flavors can deepen and blend. Nothing is more refreshing on a hot summer afternoon than a bowl of this rich tomato-y taste of the garden!

☻ Serves 6 (1 cup)

> 3 cups Healthy Request tomato juice or any reduced-sodium
>   tomato juice
> 1½ cups chopped unpeeled cucumber
> ½ cup chopped green bell pepper
> ½ cup chopped onion
> 1½ cups peeled and chopped tomato
> ½ cup Kraft Fat Free French Dressing
> 1 teaspoon chili seasoning
> 2 teaspoons dried parsley flakes
> ⅛ teaspoon black pepper

In a large bowl, combine tomato juice, cucumber, green pepper, onion, and tomato. Stir in French dressing, chili seasoning, parsley flakes, and black pepper. Cover and refrigerate for at least 2 hours. Gently stir again just before serving.

HINT: Good served topped with 1 tablespoon fat-free sour cream, but don't forget to count the few additional calories.

Each serving equals:

HE: 2⅓ Vegetable • ¼ Slider • 13 Optional Calories

64 Calories • 0 gm Fat • 2 gm Protein •
14 gm Carbohydrate • 302 mg Sodium •
18 mg Calcium • 2 gm Fiber

DIABETIC: 2 Vegetable • ½ Starch

Easy Minestrone Soup

In Italian homes and restaurants, a true minestrone may cook for hours on end before it's served to an appreciative crowd. Most of us haven't got that much time, but we still long for the hearty flavors of this peasant classic. Now, through the wizardry of the microwave, we can prepare it in less than half an hour—and the result is *delicioso!* ☻ Serves 4 (1 cup)

½ cup chopped onion
½ cup shredded carrots
½ cup chopped celery
1¾ cups (one 15-ounce can) Swanson Beef Broth ☆
1 cup (one 8-ounce can) Hunt's Tomato Sauce
1 teaspoon Italian seasoning

6 ounces (one 8-ounce can) red kidney beans, rinsed and drained
1¼ cups water
⅔ cup (1½ ounces) uncooked macaroni
½ cup chopped unpeeled zucchini
¼ cup (¾ ounce) grated Kraft fat-free Parmesan cheese

In an 8-cup glass measuring bowl, combine onion, carrots, celery, and ¼ cup beef broth. Cover and microwave on HIGH (100% power) for 3 to 4 minutes, or until vegetables are tender. Stir in tomato sauce, Italian seasoning, kidney beans, remaining 1½ cups beef broth, water, and uncooked macaroni. Re-cover and continue to microwave on HIGH for 10 minutes, stirring after 5 minutes. Stir in zucchini. Remove cover and microwave on HIGH for 6 to 7 minutes or until macaroni is tender. When serving, sprinkle 1 tablespoon Parmesan cheese over top of each bowl.

Each serving equals:

HE: 2 Vegetable • 1 Protein • ½ Bread • 8 Optional Calories

173 Calories • 1 gm Fat • 8 gm Protein • 33 gm Carbohydrate • 898 mg Sodium • 45 mg Calcium • 6 gm Fiber

DIABETIC: 2 Vegetable • 1 Meat • 1 Starch

Minestrone Noodle Soup

This sturdy peasant soup brings all your fresh vegetables together in one soothing pot, then adds both beans and noodles to give it substance and lots of hearty nourishment. It's high in fiber, low in calories, and jam-packed with goodness.

⊙ Serves 4 (1½ cups)

> 1¾ cups (one 14½-ounce can) Swanson Beef Broth
> 1 cup Healthy Request tomato juice or any reduced-sodium
>   tomato juice
> 1 cup water
> 1 cup shredded cabbage
> ¾ cup sliced celery
> ¾ cup sliced carrots
> ½ cup chopped onion
> 1 cup peeled and chopped fresh tomatoes
> 1 teaspoon dried parsley flakes
> Scant 1 cup (1½ ounces) uncooked noodles
> 6 ounces (one 8-ounce can) red kidney beans, rinsed and drained

In a large saucepan, combine beef broth, tomato juice, and water. Add cabbage, celery, carrots, onion, tomatoes, and parsley flakes. Mix well to combine. Bring mixture to a boil. Stir in uncooked noodles and kidney beans. Lower heat, cover, and simmer for 20 minutes or until vegetables are tender, stirring occasionally.

Each serving equals:

HE: 2½ Vegetable • ¾ Protein •
½ Bread • 8 Optional Calories

92 Calories • 0 gm Fat • 4 gm Protein •
19 gm Carbohydrate • 76 mg Sodium •
47 mg Calcium • 5 gm Fiber

DIABETIC: 2 Vegetable • 1 Starch • ½ Meat

Hearty Borscht

Whenever Cliff and I go out for dinner to an old-fashioned buffet restaurant not far from DeWitt, I always head for the salad bar—and the cold beets! Their beautiful color is part of their appeal, but it's their flavor that will win your heart. I especially like this supremely satisfying version that blends cabbage and potatoes with this rosy and nourishing vegetable.

◑ Serves 4 (1¼ cups)

> 1¾ cups (one 15-ounce can) Swanson Beef Broth
> 2 tablespoons lemon juice
> 2 cups (one 16-ounce can) beets, coarsely chopped and drained,
>   and ¼ cup juice reserved
> 1½ cups shredded cabbage
> ½ cup chopped onion
> 2 teaspoons pourable Sugar Twin
> 1½ cups (8 ounces) diced cooked potatoes
> ¼ cup Land O Lakes no-fat sour cream

In a large saucepan, combine beef broth, lemon juice, and reserved beet juice. Bring mixture to a boil. Stir in beets, cabbage, onion, and Sugar Twin. Lower heat and simmer for about 15 minutes or until cabbage is tender, stirring occasionally. Add potatoes. Mix well to combine. Continue simmering until potatoes are heated through, stirring occasionally. When serving, top each bowl with 1 tablespoon sour cream.

Each serving equals:

HE: 2 Vegetable • ½ Bread • ¼ Slider •
4 Optional Calories

105 Calories • 1 gm Fat • 4 gm Protein •
20 gm Carbohydrate • 430 mg Sodium •
50 mg Calcium • 3 gm Fiber

DIABETIC: 1½ Vegetable • 1 Starch

Celery-Cabbage Soup

This soup has a wonderfully old-fashioned flavor, with its blend of two good-for-you vegetables and the tangy taste of caraway seeds (the ones you find in *true* rye bread). It's a great dish to enjoy when you're feeling hungry because it's low in calories but high in tummy-filling pleasure! ☻ Serves 4 (1¼ cups)

2½ cups shredded cabbage
1 cup finely chopped celery
1½ cups water
1 (10¾-ounce) can Healthy Request Cream of Celery Soup
1 cup skim milk
¼ teaspoon caraway seed
¼ teaspoon black pepper

In a medium saucepan, combine cabbage, celery, and water. Bring mixture to a boil. Lower heat, cover, and simmer for 15 minutes or until vegetables are just tender. Add celery soup, skim milk, caraway seed, and black pepper. Mix well to combine. Continue simmering for 5 minutes or until mixture is heated through, stirring occasionally.

Each serving equals:

HE: 1¾ Vegetable • ¼ Skim Milk •
½ Slider • 1 Optional Calorie

82 Calories • 2 gm Fat • 3 gm Protein •
13 gm Carbohydrate • 365 mg Sodium •
159 mg Calcium • 1 gm Fiber

DIABETIC: ½ Vegetable • ½ Starch

Cheddar Broccoli Noodle Soup

Some relationships just seem perfect from the start, don't they? That's certainly true with broccoli and cheddar cheese! The trick was creating a cheesy broccoli combo that whisked out most of the fat—and kept the irresistible flavor. Everyone who tried this soup gave it 10 stars, so I hope you will too. ☻ Serves 4 (1¼ cups)

2 cups (one 16-ounce can) Healthy Request Chicken Broth
1½ cups water
½ cup chopped onion
1 (10-ounce) package frozen chopped broccoli, thawed
Scant 1 cup (1½ ounces) uncooked noodles
1½ cups (one 12-fluid-ounce can) Carnation Evaporated Skim Milk
3 tablespoons all-purpose flour
¾ cup (3 ounces) shredded Kraft reduced-fat Cheddar cheese
¼ teaspoon lemon pepper

In a large saucepan, combine chicken broth, water, onion, and broccoli. Bring mixture to a boil, stirring occasionally. Add uncooked noodles. Mix well to combine. Continue cooking for 10 to 12 minutes or until noodles are tender. In a covered jar, combine evaporated skim milk and flour. Shake well to blend. Add milk mixture, Cheddar cheese, and lemon pepper to soup mixture. Mix well to combine. Lower heat and simmer for 6 to 8 minutes or until mixture is heated through and cheese melts, stirring occasionally.

HINT: Thaw broccoli by placing in a colander and rinsing under hot water for one minute.

Each serving equals:

HE: 1¾ Vegetable • 1 Protein • ¾ Skim Milk • ¾ Bread • 8 Optional Calories

284 Calories • 4 gm Fat • 20 gm Protein • 42 gm Carbohydrate • 550 mg Sodium • 461 mg Calcium • 3 gm Fiber

DIABETIC: 1½ Vegetable • 1 Meat • 1 Skim Milk • ½ Starch

French Cauliflower Soup

Here's a funny bit of trivia for you: did you know that the French sometimes call their loved ones *"mon petit chou-fleur"*—my little cauliflower? I thought of that while I was stirring up this soul-satisfying soup, and decided it was just the dish to serve to the people you love! ☻ Serves 4 (1¼ cups)

2 cups (one 16-ounce can)
    Healthy Request
    Chicken Broth
1 cup water
3 cups chopped fresh
    cauliflower
⅔ cup (2 ounces) uncooked
    Minute Rice
½ cup finely chopped celery

1½ cups (one 12-fluid-ounce
    can) Carnation
    Evaporated Skim Milk
3 tablespoons all-purpose
    flour
½ teaspoon lemon pepper
2 tablespoons fresh snipped
    parsley or 2 teaspoons
    dried parsley flakes

In a large saucepan, combine chicken broth, water, cauliflower, uncooked rice, and celery. Bring mixture to a boil. Lower heat, cover, and simmer for 15 minutes or until cauliflower and rice are tender, stirring occasionally. In a covered jar, combine evaporated skim milk, flour, and lemon pepper. Shake well to blend. Add milk mixture to soup mixture. Mix well to combine. Continue simmering until mixture thickens, stirring occasionally. When serving, garnish each bowl with 1½ teaspoons parsley.

Each serving equals:

HE: 1¾ Vegetable • ¾ Skim Milk • ¾ Bread • 8 Optional Calories

152 Calories • 0 gm Fat • 12 gm Protein • 26 gm Carbohydrate • 387 mg Sodium • 306 mg Calcium • 2 gm Fiber

DIABETIC: 1 Vegetable • 1 Skim Milk • 1 Starch

Corn Rice Chowder

✳

There's something so warming about corn chowder, isn't there? So thick and rich, so creamy and flavorful, you worry it's *too good* to be good for you. Here's a version that couldn't be simpler, but packs a real wallop of taste and nourishment!   ◑   Serves 4 (1 cup)

½ cup chopped onion
1 cup diced celery
2 cups (one 16-ounce can)
    Healthy Request Chicken
    Broth
1½ cups (one 12-fluid-ounce
    can) Carnation
    Evaporated Skim Milk

3 tablespoons all-purpose flour
1 cup frozen whole-kernel
    corn, thawed
⅓ cup (1 ounce) uncooked
    Minute Rice
2 tablespoons Hormel Bacon Bits
1 teaspoon dried parsley flakes
¼ teaspoon black pepper

In a large saucepan, combine onion, celery, and chicken broth. Bring mixture to a boil. Lower heat, cover, and simmer for 10 minutes or until vegetables are tender. In a covered jar, combine evaporated skim milk and flour. Shake well to blend. Add milk mixture to broth mixture. Mix well to combine. Stir in corn, uncooked rice, bacon bits, parsley flakes, and black pepper. Re-cover and continue simmering for about 10 minutes or until mixture is heated through and rice is tender, stirring occasionally.

HINT: Thaw corn by placing in a colander and rinsing under hot
    water for one minute.

Each serving equals:

HE: 1 Bread • ¾ Skim Milk • ¾ Vegetable •
¼ Slider • 1 Optional Calorie

181 Calories • 1 gm Fat • 13 gm Protein •
30 gm Carbohydrate • 505 mg Sodium •
298 mg Calcium • 2 gm Fiber

DIABETIC: 1½ Starch • 1 Skim Milk

Chinese Corn Chowder

Many Chinese restaurants feature a creamy corn soup, so I thought this cookbook ought to offer you a tangy, healthy version! I think you'll be surprised and pleased how much color and taste the lettuce adds to this dish.   ☻   Serves 4 (1 cup)

> 2 cups (one 16-ounce can) whole-kernel corn, undrained
> 1 (10¾-ounce) can Healthy Request Cream of Mushroom Soup
> 1 tablespoon La Choy Reduced Sodium Soy Sauce
> ½ cup (one 2.5-ounce jar) sliced mushrooms, undrained
> 1 cup skim milk
> 1 cup finely shredded iceberg lettuce

In a large saucepan, combine undrained corn, mushroom soup, soy sauce, and undrained mushrooms. Bring mixture just to boiling. Lower heat and simmer for 5 minutes. Add skim milk and lettuce. Mix well to combine. Remove from heat. Serve at once.

Each serving equals:

HE: 1 Bread • ¾ Vegetable • ¼ Skim Milk •
½ Slider, 1 Optional Calorie

145 Calories • 1 gm Fat • 6 gm Protein •
28 gm Carbohydrate • 545 mg Sodium •
132 mg Calcium • 3 gm Fiber

DIABETIC: 1½ Starch/Carbohydrate • 1 Vegetable

Italian Comfort Soup

There are so many hearty peasant-type soups served in the Italian countryside, where the gifts of the harvest turn up in nearly every dish you try! This recipe is as soothing as it is sensationally flavorful—and oh-so-good for you too. ☻ Serves 4 (1¼ cups)

3 cups water

10 ounces (one 16-ounce can) great northern beans, rinsed and drained ☆

1 (10¾-ounce) can Healthy Request Cream of Mushroom Soup

1 teaspoon Italian seasoning

¼ teaspoon dried minced garlic

½ cup chopped onion

1½ cups (8 ounces) diced cooked potatoes

1 cup cooked elbow macaroni, rinsed and drained

¼ cup (¾ ounce) grated Kraft fat-free Parmesan cheese

Place water and ½ cup great northern beans in a blender container. Cover and process on HIGH for 15 seconds or until blended. Pour mixture into a large saucepan. Stir in the remaining great northern beans and mushroom soup. Add Italian seasoning, garlic, and onion. Mix well to combine. Bring mixture to a boil. Stir in potatoes and macaroni. Lower heat, cover, and simmer for 15 minutes or until mixture is heated through, stirring occasionally. When serving, sprinkle 1 tablespoon Parmesan cheese over top of each bowl.

HINT: ⅔ cup uncooked macaroni usually cooks to about 1 cup.

Each serving equals:

HE: 1½ Protein • 1 Bread • ¼ Vegetable • ½ Slider • 1 Optional Calorie

234 Calories • 2 gm Fat • 10 gm Protein • 44 gm Carbohydrate • 385 mg Sodium • 109 mg Calcium • 6 gm Fiber

DIABETIC: 2½ Starch • 1 Meat

Quick Cream of Pea Soup

Here's another great example of the power of pureeing when it comes to preparing a scrumptious cream soup without the extra fat of real cream! This dish turns a beautiful pale green color when you blend the peas and milk together, and truly feeds the eye as well as the taste buds.　　❍　　Serves 4 (1 cup)

¼ cup finely chopped onion
¼ cup finely chopped celery
1½ cups frozen peas, thawed
1 cup skim milk
3 tablespoons all-purpose flour
2 cups (one 16-ounce can) Healthy Request Chicken Broth
1 full cup (6 ounces) diced Dubuque 97% fat-free ham or any
　　extra-lean ham

In a medium saucepan sprayed with butter-flavored cooking spray, sauté onion and celery for 10 minutes or until tender. In a blender container, combine peas, skim milk, and flour. Cover and process on PUREE for 20 seconds or until mixture is smooth. Pour pea mixture into saucepan with vegetables. Add chicken broth and ham. Mix well to combine. Continue cooking for 6 to 8 minutes or until mixture is heated through, stirring often.

HINT:　Thaw peas by placing in a colander and rinsing under hot water for one minute.

Each serving equals:

HE: 1 Bread • 1 Protein • ¼ Skim Milk •
¼ Vegetable • 8 Optional Calories

142 Calories • 2 gm Fat • 14 gm Protein •
17 gm Carbohydrate • 641 mg Sodium •
95 mg Calcium • 3 gm Fiber

DIABETIC: 1 Starch • 1 Meat

Baked Potato Soup

Baked potato skins are probably the most popular restaurant appetizer, ordered for just about any occasion. But filled with cheese and bacon, they are among the most unhealthy snacks ever invented! I, of course, took that as a challenge, and came up with a soup that features those much-loved flavors but is just as good *for* you as it is GOOD GOOD GOOD!   ☻   Serves 4 (1 cup)

¼ cup chopped onion

1 (10¾-ounce) can Healthy Request Cream of Mushroom Soup

1½ cups (one 12-fluid-ounce can) Carnation Evaporated Skim Milk

2 full cups (12 ounces) diced, unpeeled baked russet potatoes

¼ cup Hormel Bacon Bits

¾ cup (3 ounces) shredded Kraft reduced-fat Cheddar cheese

¼ cup chopped green onion

In a large saucepan sprayed with butter-flavored cooking spray, sauté onion for 5 minutes or until tender. Add mushroom soup, evaporated skim milk, potatoes, and bacon bits. Mix well to combine. Lower heat and simmer for 10 minutes, stirring occasionally. Stir in Cheddar cheese and green onion. Continue simmering for 5 minutes or until cheese melts, stirring often.

Each serving equals:

HE: 1 Protein • ¾ Skim Milk • ¾ Bread •
¼ Vegetable • ¾ Slider • 6 Optional Calories

263 Calories • 7 gm Fat • 18 gm Protein •
32 gm Carbohydrate • 843 mg Sodium •
477 mg Calcium • 1 gm Fiber

DIABETIC: 1 Meat • 1 Skim Milk • 1 Starch

Homeland Potato Soup

I've always got a can or two of sauerkraut on my pantry shelves because Cliff and I find it adds so much to so many dishes. (Our favorite pizza place even features a pizza with sauerkraut in the topping!) This hearty potato soup is creamy and tangy, and perfect for serving to a crowd watching football on a Sunday afternoon.

◑   Serves 4 (1½ cups)

> 1 cup finely chopped celery
> ½ cup finely chopped onion
> 1 (10¾-ounce) can Healthy Request Cream of Celery Soup
> 1 cup (one 8-ounce can) sauerkraut, well drained
> 1⅓ cups skim milk
> 1 tablespoon pourable Sugar Twin
> ¼ cup Hormel Bacon Bits
> 1½ cups (8 ounces) diced cooked potatoes

In a large saucepan sprayed with butter-flavored cooking spray, sauté celery and onion for 6 to 8 minutes or until tender. Stir in celery soup, sauerkraut, and skim milk. Add Sugar Twin, bacon bits, and potatoes. Mix well to combine. Lower heat and simmer for 10 minutes or until mixture is heated through, stirring occasionally.

Each serving equals:

HE: 1¼ Vegetable • ½ Bread • ⅓ Skim Milk • ¾ Slider • 8 Optional Calories

155 Calories • 3 gm Fat • 8 gm Protein • 24 gm Carbohydrate • 911 mg Sodium • 188 mg Calcium • 3 gm Fiber

DIABETIC: 1½ Starch/Carbohydrate • 1 Meat

Grandma's Potato Soup with Cheese Dumplings

I don't know about you, but if I saw this recipe name on a restaurant menu, I'd be ready to order in two seconds! This dish was inspired by my mother's creamy-rich potato soup, and the dumplings make it even more of a treat. Serve this on a chilly winter evening, and you'll have sweet dreams all night long.

○ Serves 4 (1 cup soup and 1 dumpling)

2 cups hot water
2 cups (10 ounces) diced raw potatoes
½ cup chopped onion
1 cup chopped celery
1½ cups (one 12-fluid-ounce can) Carnation Evaporated Skim Milk
¼ teaspoon lemon pepper
6 tablespoons Bisquick Reduced Fat Baking Mix
1 teaspoon dried parsley flakes
1 teaspoon dried onion flakes
3 tablespoons (¾ ounce) shredded Kraft reduced-fat Cheddar cheese
¼ cup skim milk

In a large saucepan, combine water, potatoes, onion, and celery. Bring mixture to a boil. Lower heat, cover, and simmer for 15 minutes or until vegetables are tender. Add evaporated skim milk and lemon pepper. Mix well to combine. In a small bowl, combine baking mix, parsley flakes, onion flakes, and Cheddar cheese. Add skim milk. Mix gently just to combine. Drop batter by tablespoonful into hot mixture to form 4 dumplings. Cover and continue simmering for 10 to 15 minutes or until dumplings are firm.

HINT: I left the peels on the potatoes, but you can peel them if you prefer.

Each serving equals:

HE: 1 Bread • ¾ Skim Milk • ¾ Vegetable •
¼ Protein • 6 Optional Calories

194 Calories • 2 gm Fat • 12 gm Protein •
32 gm Carbohydrate • 324 mg Sodium •
363 mg Calcium • 2 gm Fiber

DIABETIC: 1 Starch • 1 Skim Milk

Mexican Macaroni Chowder ❄

We use a lot of salsa in our house, and I keep two kinds (at least!) on hand. Cliff is happiest when the smoke is pouring out of his ears, while I prefer the fresh flavor of tomatoes and onions without those "call-the-fire-department" hot chilis. My suggestion for this recipe: start out mild, and offer a dish of the spicy stuff for anyone whose taste buds like to sizzle the way Cliff's do!

◐ Serves 4 (1¼ cups)

½ cup chunky salsa (mild, medium, or hot)

1 (10¾-ounce) can Healthy Request Tomato Soup

2 cups Healthy Request tomato juice or any reduced-sodium tomato juice

1½ teaspoons chili seasoning

1 teaspoon dried parsley flakes

1 cup hot cooked elbow macaroni, rinsed and drained

½ cup frozen whole-kernel corn, thawed

¾ cup (3 ounces) shredded Kraft reduced-fat Cheddar cheese

In a large saucepan, combine salsa, tomato soup, and tomato juice. Stir in chili seasoning and parsley flakes. Bring mixture to a boil. Add macaroni, corn, and Cheddar cheese. Mix well to combine. Lower heat and simmer for 6 to 8 minutes or until mixture is heated through and cheese is melted, stirring occasionally.

HINTS: 1. ⅔ cup uncooked elbow macaroni usually cooks to about 1 cup.

2. Thaw corn by placing in a colander and rinsing under hot water for one minute.

Each serving equals:

HE: 1¼ Vegetable • 1 Protein • ¾ Bread • ½ Slider • 5 Optional Calories

---

196 Calories • 4 gm Fat • 10 gm Protein • 30 gm Carbohydrate • 532 mg Sodium • 203 mg Calcium • 2 gm Fiber

---

Fin and
Feather Soups

When I was choosing my recipes for this cookbook, I decided to combine some favorite soups that featured seafood with a bundle of scrumptious and satisfying chicken and turkey blends. *Voilà!* Fin and feather—a little old-fashioned country nickname for this category of recipes . . . not unlike the famous "surf and turf." Because so many people are cutting back on meat and incorporating more fish and poultry into their menus, I figured these two "creatures" would make a happy, healthy partnership!

Soup is a smart way to use up those little bits of leftovers cluttering your refrigerator, and in fact can inspire you in dozens of delightful ways to cook up a quick and tasty kettle of soup just about anytime at all. In fancy kitchens, they even add some water to the cooking pan and scrape out all those bits and pieces that stuck during cooking, then add that to an ever-present stockpot. I'm not suggesting you make your own chicken or turkey or fish stock, which can be very time-consuming, but I mention this so when you're planning a week's menus, you'll remember that what's left *after* a meal can form the basis of the next!

*Chicken soup to feed a cold is a popular recommendation, but please don't save these delectable recipes only for those times when you're not feeling well. You'll soon discover that the soups in this section will make you feel even better on a day when you're already feeling pretty great! Whether you're stirring chunks of chicken into a bubbling broth (***Lancaster Chicken Corn Soup with Rivels***), mixing bits of crabmeat or shrimp into a creamy chowder (***Pasta Seafood Chowder, Cajun Corn-Shrimp Soup***), or using up Thanksgiving leftovers in a way that will make your whole family truly grateful (***Turkey Tetrazzini Soup***), these recipes will soothe your soul and heal your heart. Mmm-mm!*

Fin and
Feather Soups

Tuna Noodle Chowder ❄

Are you one of those old-fashioned people who always loved tuna noodle casserole? (If you grew up in the 1950s, I'm not at all surprised!) Well, I share your affection for this well-loved classic, and so I decided to stir up a soup that celebrates it! True, there are no potato chips crumbled on top, but you could use a couple of the new fat-free ones if you like (just add the extra optional calories to each serving). ☻ Serves 4 (1 full cup)

1½ cups hot water
1 teaspoon dried onion flakes
Scant 1 cup (1½ ounces)
    uncooked noodles
½ cup frozen peas, thawed
1 (6-ounce) can white tuna,
    packed in water,
    drained and flaked
1 (10¾-ounce) can Healthy

Request Cream of
    Mushroom Soup
1 teaspoon dried parsley
    flakes
1½ cups (one 12-fluid-ounce
    can) Carnation
    Evaporated Skim Milk
⅛ teaspoon black pepper

In a large saucepan, combine water, onion flakes, and uncooked noodles. Bring mixture to a boil. Stir in peas, tuna, mushroom soup, and parsley flakes. Lower heat, cover, and simmer for about 5 minutes. Add evaporated skim milk and black pepper. Mix well to combine. Continue simmering for about 5 minutes or until mixture is heated through, stirring occasionally.

HINT: Thaw peas by placing in a colander and rinsing under hot water for one minute.

Each serving equals:

HE: ¾ Skim Milk • ¾ Bread • ¾ Protein •
½ Slider • 1 Optional Calorie

231 Calories • 3 gm Fat • 21 gm Protein •
30 gm Carbohydrate • 558 mg Sodium •
344 mg Calcium • 2 gm Fiber

DIABETIC: 1½ Starch • 1½ Meat • 1 Skim Milk

Deep Sea Chowder

Creamy, cheesy, and wonderfully rich, this soup is a dream come true for people who love the delicate flavor of fish! Those chunks of potato provide so much tummy satisfaction, no one will believe this dish is part of a healthy eating plan!

○ Serves 4 (1 full cup)

¾ cup finely diced celery
¼ cup finely chopped onion
1 (10¾-ounce) can Healthy Request Cream of Celery Soup
1½ cups (one 12-fluid-ounce can) Carnation Evaporated Skim
    Milk
¾ cup (3 ounces) shredded Kraft reduced-fat Cheddar cheese
1 (6-ounce) can white tuna, packed in water, drained and flaked
1½ cups (8 ounces) diced cooked potatoes
¼ cup (one 2-ounce jar) chopped pimiento, undrained
1 teaspoon dried parsley flakes
⅛ teaspoon black pepper

In a large saucepan sprayed with butter-flavored cooking spray, sauté celery and onion for 5 minutes or until tender. Stir in celery soup and evaporated skim milk. Add Cheddar cheese, tuna, potatoes, undrained pimiento, parsley flakes, and black pepper. Mix well to combine. Lower heat and simmer for 10 minutes or until mixture is heated through and cheese melts, stirring often.

Each serving equals:

HE: 1¾ Protein • ¾ Skim Milk • ½ Bread •
½ Vegetable • ½ Slider • 1 Optional Calorie

262 Calories • 6 gm Fat • 25 gm Protein •
27 gm Carbohydrate • 755 mg Sodium •
489 mg Calcium • 1 gm Fiber

DIABETIC: 2 Meat • 1 Skim Milk • 1 Starch

Cajun Corn-Shrimp Soup ❄

Seafood soups are a special delight in every coastal area, but perhaps nowhere more adored than in the bayous of Louisiana, where every kind of shellfish is honored with spicy recipes all its own! This quick-to-fix dish incorporates easy-to-find ingredients that will make you feel like "letting the good times roll"!

◑ Serves 4 (1¼ cups)

¼ cup finely chopped onion

1¾ cups (one 14½-ounce can) stewed tomatoes, undrained

1 (10¾-ounce) can Healthy Request Tomato Soup

1 cup water

2 cups frozen whole-kernel corn, thawed

1 teaspoon Cajun seasoning

1 teaspoon dried parsley flakes

1 (4.5-ounce drained weight) can small shrimp, rinsed and drained

In a large saucepan sprayed with butter-flavored cooking spray, sauté onion for about 5 minutes or until tender. Stir in undrained tomatoes, tomato soup, and water. Add corn, Cajun seasoning, and parsley flakes. Mix well to combine. Bring mixture to a boil. Stir in shrimp. Lower heat and simmer for 10 minutes, stirring occasionally.

HINT: Thaw corn by placing in a colander and rinsing under hot water for one minute.

Each serving equals:

HE: 1 Bread • 1 Protein • 1 Vegetable • ½ Slider • 12 Optional Calories

185 Calories • 1 gm Fat • 11 gm Protein • 33 gm Carbohydrate • 604 mg Sodium • 87 mg Calcium • 4 gm Fiber

DIABETIC: 1½ Starch • 1 Meat • 1 Vegetable

Tomato Shrimp Chowder

Originally, a chowder always meant a thick seafood soup usually combined with potatoes, though these days almost any chunky soup recipe may carry the name. Here's a quick and easy classic that is just brimming with rich flavor!   ☺   Serves 4 (1 cup)

> 1¼ cups finely chopped celery
> ¼ cup finely chopped onion
> 1 (10¾-ounce) can Healthy Request Tomato Soup
> 1⅓ cups skim milk
> 1 teaspoon seafood seasoning
> 1 (4.5-ounce drained weight) can medium shrimp, rinsed and
>   drained
> 1½ cups (8 ounces) diced cooked potatoes

In a large saucepan sprayed with butter-flavored cooking spray, sauté celery and onion for 8 to 10 minutes, or until tender. Stir in tomato soup, skim milk, and seafood seasoning. Add shrimp and potatoes. Mix well to combine. Lower heat and simmer for 10 minutes, stirring occasionally.

Each serving equals:

HE: 1 Protein • ¾ Vegetable • ½ Bread •
⅓ Skim Milk • ½ Slider • 12 Optional Calories

158 Calories • 2 gm Fat • 12 gm Protein •
23 gm Carbohydrate • 361 mg Sodium •
148 mg Calcium • 2 gm Fiber

DIABETIC: 1½ Starch/Carbohydrate •
1 Meat • ½ Vegetable

Quick Clam Chowder

This dish used to be a mainstay of every coffee shop and family restaurant on every Friday throughout the year! Now you can serve up a delicious version that's prepared in your microwave but tastes like it cooked for hours on an old-fashioned stove.

○ Serves 4 (¾ cup)

1 (4.5-ounce drained weight) can minced clams, undrained
1 cup (5 ounces) diced raw potatoes
¼ cup diced onion
¼ cup diced celery
½ cup water
2 tablespoons Hormel Bacon Bits

1 teaspoon dried parsley flakes
2 teaspoons reduced-calorie margarine
¼ teaspoon black pepper
1½ cups (one 12-fluid-ounce can) Carnation Evaporated Skim Milk
3 tablespoons all-purpose flour

In an 8-cup glass measuring bowl, combine undrained clams, potatoes, onion, celery, and water. Cover and microwave on HIGH (100% power) for 6 to 8 minutes or until potatoes are tender. Stir in bacon bits, parsley flakes, margarine, and black pepper. In a small bowl, combine evaporated skim milk and flour. Add milk mixture to clam mixture. Mix well to combine. Re-cover and continue microwaving on HIGH for 2 to 3 minutes or just until mixture starts to boil. Let set 2 minutes. Stir well just before serving.

Each serving equals:

HE: 1 Protein • ¾ Skim Milk • ½ Bread •
¼ Fat • ¼ Vegetable • ¼ Slider

166 Calories • 2 gm Fat • 14 gm Protein •
23 gm Carbohydrate • 304 mg Sodium •
306 mg Calcium • 1 gm Fiber

DIABETIC: 1 Meat • 1 Skim Milk • ½ Starch

Pasta Seafood Chowder

If your idea of heaven is a thick and luscious cream soup, this one will send your taste buds flying sky high! I think it's extra-special with crabmeat, but for variety, try making it with shrimp.

● Serves 4 (1¼ cups)

¾ cup sliced fresh mushrooms
2 cups skim milk
1 (10¾-ounce) can Healthy Request Cream of Mushroom Soup
¼ cup sliced green onion
1 cup cooked shell macaroni, rinsed and drained
2 (4-ounce drained weight) cans crabmeat or frozen imitation
*   crab, thawed*
2 tablespoons chopped fresh parsley
1 teaspoon seafood seasoning

In a large saucepan sprayed with butter-flavored cooking spray, sauté mushrooms for 3 minutes, stirring constantly. Add milk and mushroom soup. Mix well to combine. Stir in green onion, macaroni, crabmeat, parsley, and seafood seasoning. Lower heat and simmer for 6 to 8 minutes or until mixture is heated through, stirring often. Serve immediately.

HINT: ⅔ cup uncooked shell macaroni usually cooks to about 1 cup.

Each serving equals:

HE: 2 Protein • ½ Skim Milk • ½ Bread •
½ Vegetable • ¼ Slider • 5 Optional Calories

203 Calories • 3 gm Fat • 19 gm Protein •
25 gm Carbohydrate • 680 mg Sodium •
275 mg Calcium • 2 gm Fiber

DIABETIC: 2 Meat • 1 Skim Milk • 1 Starch

Chicken Soup Almondine

Talk about luscious! Mmm-mm, this creamy chicken soup is sinfully rich, and the almonds add great flavor and texture to a dish that's already a surefire winner. This is a lovely soup to serve at a dinner party—easy to prepare but a true taste of luxury!

○ Serves 4 (1 cup)

1 (10¾-ounce) can Healthy Request Cream of Chicken Soup
2 cups (one 16-ounce can) Healthy Request Chicken Broth
⅓ cup Carnation Nonfat Dry Milk Powder
¼ cup (1 ounce) sliced almonds
1 teaspoon dried parsley flakes
1 cup (5 ounces) chopped cooked chicken breast

In a medium saucepan, combine chicken soup, chicken broth, and dry milk powder. Stir in almonds and parsley flakes. Add chicken. Mix well to combine. Cook over medium heat for about 10 minutes or until mixture is heated through, stirring often.

HINT: If you don't have leftovers, purchase a chunk of cooked chicken breast from your local deli.

Each serving equals:

HE: 1½ Protein • ½ Fat • ¼ Skim Milk •
½ Slider • 13 Optional Calories

170 Calories • 6 gm Fat • 17 gm Protein •
12 gm Carbohydrate • 598 mg Sodium •
95 mg Calcium • 1 gm Fiber

DIABETIC: 1½ Meat • 1 Starch • ½ Fat

Superb Cream of Chicken Soup ❄

Don't you just love a dish that combines luscious flavor with preparation so simple you only have one dish to wash? (Anyone who knows me knows this is my idea of heaven!) Healthy cream soups are a passion of mine, and this one will convince you that you're enjoying something forbidden—but trust me, you're still riding the Health Wagon!   ☻   Serves 4 (1 cup)

1 (10¾-ounce) can Healthy Request Cream of Chicken Soup
1⅓ cups skim milk
¼ cup (¾ ounce) grated Kraft fat-free Parmesan cheese
¼ cup (one 2-ounce jar) chopped pimiento, undrained
¼ cup (1 ounce) sliced ripe olives
1 teaspoon dried parsley flakes
1 cup (5 ounces) chopped cooked chicken breast

In an 8-cup glass measuring bowl, combine chicken soup and skim milk. Add Parmesan cheese, undrained pimiento, olives, and parsley flakes. Mix well to combine. Stir in chicken. Cover and microwave on HIGH (100% power) for 3 to 4 minutes, or until mixture is heated through. Stir well before serving.

HINT: If you don't have leftovers, purchase a chunk of cooked chicken breast from your local deli.

Each serving equals:

HE: 1½ Protein • ⅓ Skim Milk • ¼ Fat •
½ Slider • 5 Optional Calories

135 Calories • 3 gm Fat • 15 gm Protein •
12 gm Carbohydrate • 463 mg Sodium •
115 mg Calcium • 1 gm Fiber

DIABETIC: 1½ Meat • 1 Starch

Chicken-Vegetable Soup Pot   ❄

Do you remember learning about the Presidential campaign promise of "a chicken in every pot"? If the candidate delivered that speech, and then handed out this recipe, he'd definitely win my vote—and yours, too, I'll bet!   ☻   Serves 6 (1½ cups)

> 2 full cups (12 ounces) diced cooked chicken breast
> 2 cups (one 16-ounce can) Healthy Request Chicken Broth
> 3½ cups water
> 1 teaspoon lemon pepper
> 2 teaspoons dried parsley flakes
> ½ cup chopped onion
> 1½ cups finely diced celery
> 1½ cups finely chopped carrots
> 1 cup (two 2.5-ounce jars) sliced mushrooms, drained

In a slow cooker container, combine chicken, chicken broth, water, lemon pepper, and parsley flakes. Stir in onion, celery, carrots, and mushrooms. Cover and cook on LOW for 8 hours. Stir well before serving.

HINTS: 1. If you don't have leftovers, purchase a chunk of cooked chicken breast from your local deli.
2. If you don't have a slow cooker, you can simmer in a large covered saucepan for 30 minutes.

Each serving equals:

HE: 2 Protein • 1½ Vegetable • 5 Optional Calories

126 Calories • 2 gm Fat • 20 gm Protein •
7 gm Carbohydrate • 353 mg Sodium •
38 mg Calcium • 2 gm Fiber

DIABETIC: 2 Meat • 1 Vegetable

Creamy Chicken and Celery Soup

I think chicken and celery are a naturally delightful combination, and when you stir them into an already creamy broth, you've got the kind of tummy-pleaser that appeals to kids of all ages! This soup could also be prepared with leftover turkey for a slightly different but still delectable flavor. ☻ Serves 4 (1½ cups)

> 2 cups (one 16-ounce can) Healthy Request Chicken Broth
> 1 cup water
> ½ cup chopped onion
> ½ cup shredded carrots
> 3 cups diced celery
> 1 cup (5 ounces) diced cooked chicken breast
> 1 (10¾-ounce) can Healthy Request Cream of Chicken Soup
> 1 teaspoon dried parsley flakes
> ⅛ teaspoon black pepper

In a large saucepan, combine chicken broth, water, onion, carrots, and celery. Bring mixture to a boil. Stir in chicken. Lower heat, cover, and simmer for 15 minutes or until vegetables are tender. Add chicken soup, parsley flakes, and black pepper. Mix well to combine. Continue simmering for about 6 to 8 minutes or until mixture is heated through, stirring occasionally.

HINT: If you don't have leftovers, purchase a chunk of cooked chicken breast from your local deli.

Each serving equals:

HE: 2 Vegetable • 1¼ Protein • ½ Slider •
13 Optional Calories

139 Calories • 3 gm Fat • 14 gm Protein •
14 gm Carbohydrate • 650 mg Sodium •
51 mg Calcium • 2 gm Fiber

DIABETIC: 1 Vegetable • 1 Meat • 1 Starch

Lancaster Chicken Corn Soup with Rivels

Inspired by the cooking traditions of the Pennsylvania Dutch ("rivels" are a cross between a dumpling and a noodle), this hearty chicken soup is so substantial, you could enjoy it as a main dish, accompanied by a salad and some fresh fruit. Be sure to wash your hands carefully after handling the raw egg—safety first!

⊘   Serves 4 (1½ cups)

> 4 cups (two 16-ounce cans) Healthy Request Chicken Broth
> 1 cup water
> 1 full cup (6 ounces) diced cooked chicken breast
> 1½ cups frozen whole-kernel corn, thawed
> 1 teaspoon dried parsley flakes
> ¼ teaspoon black pepper
> 1 cup all-purpose flour
> 1 egg or equivalent in egg substitute
> 1 hard-boiled egg, chopped

In a large saucepan, combine chicken broth, water, chicken, corn, parsley flakes, and black pepper. Bring mixture to a boil. Lower heat and simmer for 3 to 4 minutes. Meanwhile in a medium bowl, combine flour and raw egg. To make rivels, mix flour mixture by hand until it is the consistency of pie dough crumbs. Slowly add rivels to boiling soup by crumbling into soup with one hand while constantly stirring with the other hand. Continue simmering for about 5 minutes, stirring occasionally. Fold in chopped egg. Serve at once.

HINTS: 1. If you don't have leftovers, purchase a chunk of cooked chicken breast from your local deli.
2. Thaw corn by placing in a colander and rinsing under hot water for one minute.

Each serving equals:

HE: 2 Bread • 2 Protein (½ limited) •
¼ Slider • 2 Optional Calories

---

288 Calories • 4 gm Fat • 25 gm Protein •
38 gm Carbohydrate • 547 mg Sodium •
27 mg Calcium • 3 gm Fiber

DIABETIC: 2 Starch • 2 Meat

Chicken Burrito Soup ❄

I stirred up this dish to surprise my husband, Cliff, who loves anything Mexican—even soup! I left out the tortillas, but you'll see I included just about everything else that makes burritos such a popular choice. This soup is colorful, full of flavor, and fills your house with a wonderful spicy fragrance.   ☺   Serves 4 (1½ cups)

2 cups (one 16-ounce can) Healthy Request Chicken Broth
1 cup water
2 teaspoons taco seasoning
¼ teaspoon dried minced garlic
1 teaspoon dried parsley flakes
1 cup frozen whole-kernel corn, thawed
¼ cup chopped red bell pepper
¼ cup chopped green bell pepper
½ cup chopped onion
1 cup (5 ounces) diced cooked chicken breast
6 ounces (one 8-ounce can) red kidney beans, rinsed and drained
1 cup (one 8-ounce can) stewed tomatoes, coarsely chopped and
*   undrained*
Scant 1 cup (1½ ounces) uncooked noodles

In a large saucepan, combine chicken broth, water, taco seasoning, garlic, and parsley flakes. Add corn, red and green peppers, onion, chicken, kidney beans, and undrained tomatoes. Mix well to combine. Bring mixture to a boil. Stir in uncooked noodles. Lower heat, cover, and simmer for about 15 minutes or until vegetables and noodles are tender, stirring occasionally.

HINTS: 1. Thaw corn by placing in a colander and rinsing under hot water for one minute.
2. If you don't have leftovers, purchase a chunk of cooked chicken breast from your local deli.

Each serving equals:

HE: 2 Protein • 1 Bread • 1 Vegetable •
8 Optional Calories

262 Calories • 2 gm Fat • 20 gm Protein •
41 gm Carbohydrate • 452 mg Sodium •
60 mg Calcium • 5 gm Fiber

DIABETIC: 2 Meat • 1½ Starch • 1 Vegetable

Old-Time Chicken Noodle Soup ❄

This is a classic, Grandma-style chicken noodle soup recipe, but even though every spoonful contains the ingredients you loved in hers, this dish cooks up fast enough to fit into every busy family's lifestyle. If you had to explain "comfort food" to people from another country, you could just give them a bowl of this!

○ Serves 4 (1½ cups)

> 4 cups (two 16-ounce cans) Healthy Request Chicken Broth
> ½ cup water
> 1 cup diced celery
> 2 cups diced carrots
> 1½ cups (8 ounces) diced cooked chicken breast
> 1 teaspoon dried parsley flakes
> ¼ teaspoon dried basil
> ⅛ teaspoon black pepper
> 1⅓ cups (2¼ ounces) uncooked noodles

In a large saucepan, combine chicken broth, water, celery, and carrots. Bring mixture to a boil. Stir in chicken, parsley flakes, basil, and black pepper. Lower heat, cover, and simmer for 15 minutes. Add uncooked noodles. Mix well to combine. Continue simmering for about 12 to 15 minutes or until noodles are tender, stirring occasionally.

HINT: If you don't have leftovers, purchase a chunk of cooked chicken breast from your local deli.

Each serving equals:

> HE: 2 Protein • 1½ Vegetable • ¾ Bread •
> 16 Optional Calories
>
> ---
>
> 283 Calories • 3 gm Fat • 27 gm Protein •
> 37 gm Carbohydrate • 571 mg Sodium •
> 46 mg Calcium • 3 gm Fiber
>
> ---
>
> DIABETIC: 2 Meat • 1 Vegetable • 1 Starch

Easy Chicken Gumbo

Traditionally, a gumbo was always made with okra, but these days the word has come to mean any thick and hearty soup jam-packed with vegetables and rich taste! I think the okra makes this a little extra-special, so if you can find some at the market, I encourage you to stir it in. ☻ Serves 4 (1⅓ cups)

> 4 cups (two 16-ounce cans) Healthy Request Chicken Broth
> 1 cup (5 ounces) diced cooked chicken breast
> ½ cup diced celery
> ½ cup chopped green bell pepper
> ½ cup chopped onion
> 1 cup sliced okra or frozen cut green beans
> 1 cup peeled and chopped fresh tomatoes
> ¼ cup (one 2-ounce jar) chopped pimiento, undrained
> ⅓ cup (1 ounce) uncooked Minute Rice

In a medium saucepan, combine chicken broth and chicken. Stir in celery, green pepper, onion, okra, tomatoes, and undrained pimiento. Bring mixture to a boil. Add uncooked rice. Mix well to combine. Lower heat, cover, and simmer for 15 minutes, stirring occasionally.

HINT: If you don't have leftovers, purchase a chunk of cooked chicken breast from your local deli.

Each serving equals:

HE: 1¾ Vegetable • 1¼ Protein •
¼ Bread • 16 Optional Calories

---

122 Calories • 2 gm Fat • 15 gm Protein •
11 gm Carbohydrate • 527 mg Sodium •
29 mg Calcium • 2 gm Fiber

DIABETIC: 1 Vegetable • 1 Meat • ½ Starch

Curried Chicken and
Corn Chowder

A friend told me about a restaurant in New York City called "Curry in a Hurry"—and that would almost be the perfect name for this yummy Indian-inspired recipe! It's wonderfully creamy, amazingly rich, and tangy with the spirit of the East. When you bite into those chunks of peanut as you spoon this one up, allow yourself to be transported in your imagination to the land of the Taj Mahal.

○ Serves 4 (1¼ cups)

> ½ cup chopped green bell pepper
> 2 cups (one 16-ounce can) cream-style corn
> 1½ cups (one 12-fluid-ounce can) Carnation Evaporated Skim
>   Milk
> 1 (10¾-ounce) can Healthy Request Cream of Chicken Soup
> 1 full cup (6 ounces) diced cooked chicken breast
> 2 teaspoons dried onion flakes
> 1 teaspoon curry powder
> ¼ cup (1 ounce) chopped dry-roasted peanuts

In a large saucepan sprayed with butter-flavored cooking spray, sauté green pepper for 5 minutes or until tender. Add corn, evaporated skim milk, chicken soup, chicken, onion flakes, and curry powder. Mix well to combine. Lower heat and simmer for 5 minutes or until mixture is heated through, stirring often. When serving, sprinkle 1 tablespoon peanuts over top of each bowl.

HINT: If you don't have leftovers, purchase a chunk of cooked
    chicken breast from your local deli.

Each serving equals:

HE: 1¾ Protein • 1 Bread • ¾ Skim Milk • ½ Fat • ¼ Vegetable • ½ Slider • 5 Optional Calories

311 Calories • 7 gm Fat • 23 gm Protein • 39 gm Carbohydrate • 791 mg Sodium • 294 mg Calcium • 2 gm Fiber

DIABETIC: 1½ Meat • 1½ Starch • 1 Skim Milk • ½ Fat

Chicken Rice Soup with Spinach

I'm not sure who first combined spinach with chicken and called it "Florentine," but it's a popular combination that's been around for many years. Here's a dish inspired by that culinary tradition, and tastiest when it's made with fresh spinach. Happily, we can find it fresh just about all year long in most of our markets.

◐ Serves 4 (1¼ cups)

> 2 cups (one 16-ounce can) Healthy Request Chicken Broth
> ¾ cup shredded carrots
> ¼ cup finely chopped onion
> 1 cup (5 ounces) diced cooked chicken breast
> 1 (10¾-ounce) can Healthy Request Cream of Chicken Soup
> 1 cup skim milk
> ⅔ cup (2 ounces) uncooked Minute Rice
> 1 cup finely shredded fresh spinach
> ¼ cup (¾ ounce) grated Kraft fat-free Parmesan cheese

In a medium saucepan, combine chicken broth, carrots, and onion. Bring mixture to a boil. Stir in chicken. Continue cooking for 5 minutes. Add chicken soup and skim milk. Mix well to combine. Stir in uncooked rice and spinach. Cover and remove from heat. Let set for 5 minutes. Stir gently. When serving, sprinkle 1 tablespoon Parmesan cheese over top of each bowl.

HINT: If you don't have leftovers, purchase a chunk of cooked chicken breast from your local deli.

Each serving equals:

> HE: 1½ Protein • 1 Vegetable • ½ Bread •
> ¼ Skim Milk • ½ Slider • 13 Optional Calories
>
> ---
>
> 187 Calories • 3 gm Fat • 17 gm Protein •
> 23 gm Carbohydrate • 691 mg Sodium •
> 97 mg Calcium • 2 gm Fiber
>
> ---
>
> DIABETIC: 1½ Meat • 1 Vegetable • 1 Starch

Heartland Chicken Pot Soup ❄

Many families have a traditional chicken soup recipe, handed down over the years, but in case you don't, I thought I'd offer a fast and flavorful version that will soon be a family favorite at your house. (My daughter Becky loves just about any chicken noodle soup!) I recommend using either the very thin noodles in this soup, or for a change (and if you prefer it), you could try flat noodles instead.

◐ Serves 4 (1½ cups)

2 cups (one 16-ounce can)
    Healthy Request
    Chicken Broth
1¾ cups water
8 ounces skinned and boned
    uncooked chicken
    breast, cut into 24
    pieces
½ cup chopped onion

1 cup thinly sliced carrots
1 cup chopped celery
1 cup (one 8-ounce can)
    Hunt's Tomato Sauce
1 teaspoon dried parsley
    flakes
¼ teaspoon black pepper
1¾ cups (3 ounces)
    uncooked noodles

In a large saucepan, combine chicken broth, water, chicken, onion, carrots, and celery. Bring mixture to a boil. Stir in tomato sauce, parsley flakes, and black pepper. Lower heat, cover, and simmer for 15 minutes, stirring occasionally. Add uncooked noodles. Mix well to combine. Continue simmering for about 8 to 10 minutes or until vegetables and noodles are tender, stirring often.

Each serving equals:

HE: 2¼ Vegetable • 1½ Protein •
1 Bread • 8 Optional Calories

266 Calories • 2 gm Fat • 22 gm Protein •
40 gm Carbohydrate • 813 mg Sodium •
42 mg Calcium • 4 gm Fiber

DIABETIC: 2 Vegetable • 1½ Meat • 1½ Starch

Chicken Stew with Bacon Dumplings

If you never learned to make dumplings at your mother's knee, don't let that discourage you from trying out this recipe on your family. Dumplings are easier than they look, they're tastier than you can imagine, and when combined here with creamy chicken, they're downright irresistible!

◑ Serves 4 (1 cup soup and 1 dumpling)

> 8 ounces skinned and boned uncooked chicken breasts, cut into 16 pieces
> 1 cup chopped onion
> 1½ cups frozen cut carrots, partially thawed
> 1 cup chopped celery
> 1 (10¾-ounce) can Healthy Request Cream of Chicken Soup
> ½ cup (one 2.5-ounce jar) sliced mushrooms, undrained
> 2 teaspoons dried parsley flakes ☆
> 1 cup skim milk ☆
> ¼ cup water
> ¾ cup Bisquick Reduced Fat Baking Mix
> ¼ cup Hormel Bacon Bits
> 1 tablespoon Land O Lakes no-fat sour cream

In a large skillet sprayed with butter-flavored cooking spray, sauté chicken, onion, carrots, and celery for 10 minutes. Stir in chicken soup, undrained mushrooms, 1 teaspoon parsley flakes, ¾ cup skim milk, and water. Lower heat, cover, and simmer for 10 minutes. In a small bowl, combine baking mix, bacon bits, remaining 1 teaspoon parsley flakes, remaining ¼ cup skim milk, and sour cream. Let batter rest for 5 minutes. Drop by tablespoonful into hot chicken mixture to form 4 dumplings. Simmer for 5 minutes, uncovered. Cover and continue simmering for 15 to 25 minutes or until dumplings are firm.

HINT: Thaw carrots by placing in a colander and rinsing under hot water for one minute.

Each serving equals:

HE: 2 Vegetable • 1½ Protein • 1 Bread •
¼ Skim Milk • ¾ Slider • 14 Optional Calories

281 Calories • 5 gm Fat • 23 gm Protein •
36 gm Carbohydrate • 852 mg Sodium •
147 mg Calcium • 3 gm Fiber

DIABETIC: 2 Starch • 1½ Meat • 1½ Vegetable

Stovetop Chicken Stew

Some nights, your family doesn't want something new and different served up for dinner. Instead, they're hoping for a cozy, traditional chicken dish that tastes like Grandma used to make. This speedy skillet stew is a simple family-pleaser I bet you'll make often.

⊙ Serves 4 (1¼ cups)

> 12 ounces skinned and boned uncooked chicken breast, cut into 12
> pieces
> 1 cup chopped onion
> 1 cup chopped celery
> 2 cups chopped cabbage
> 2 cups (one 16-ounce can) tomatoes, coarsely chopped and
> undrained
> 2 teaspoons dried parsley flakes
> ¼ teaspoon black pepper

In a large skillet sprayed with butter-flavored cooking spray, sauté chicken, onion, and celery for 10 minutes. Add cabbage, undrained tomatoes, parsley flakes, and black pepper. Mix well to combine. Bring mixture to a boil. Lower heat, cover, and simmer for 25 minutes or until chicken and vegetables are tender, stirring occasionally.

Each serving equals:

HE: 3 Vegetable • 2¼ Protein

145 Calories • 1 gm Fat • 22 gm Protein •
12 gm Carbohydrate • 284 mg Sodium •
78 mg Calcium • 3 gm Fiber

DIABETIC: 2 Vegetable • 2 Meat

Golden Turkey Noodle Soup ❄

Here's one of the reasons I enjoy the week *after* Thanksgiving almost as much as I do the week we celebrate: a hearty turkey soup just brimming with veggies and noodles. The special treat for me (and, I hope, for you) is the addition of sweet potatoes, which give the soup a luscious color.   ☻   Serves 4 (1½ cups)

> 2 cups (one 16-ounce can) Healthy Request Chicken Broth
> 1½ cups water
> ¾ cup (4 ounces) peeled and diced raw sweet potatoes
> ½ cup chopped onion
> ¾ cup shredded carrots
> ¾ cup thinly sliced celery
> 1½ cups (8 ounces) diced cooked turkey breast
> Scant 1 cup (1½ ounces) uncooked noodles
> 1 teaspoon dried parsley flakes

In a large saucepan, combine chicken broth, water, sweet potatoes, onion, carrots, and celery. Bring mixture to a boil. Lower heat, cover, and simmer for 12 to 15 minutes or until vegetables are tender, stirring occasionally. Add turkey, uncooked noodles, and parsley flakes. Mix well to combine. Continue simmering for 10 minutes or until noodles are tender, stirring occasionally.

HINT: If you don't have leftovers, purchase a chunk of cooked turkey breast from your local deli.

Each serving equals:

HE: 2 Protein • 1 Vegetable • ¾ Bread •
8 Optional Calories

158 Calories • 2 gm Fat • 21 gm Protein •
14 gm Carbohydrate • 326 mg Sodium •
36 mg Calcium • 2 gm Fiber

DIABETIC: 2 Meat • 1 Vegetable • 1 Starch

Turkey Tetrazzini Soup

✴

I first premiered a healthy turkey tetrazzini recipe in my *Healthy Exchanges Cookbook,* and it's been a popular choice ever since, especially in JO's Kitchen Cafe and at many parties we've catered. I decided to incorporate that amazing flavor into a hearty soup that's just as easy to prepare . . . and just as appealing!

☻ Serves 4 (1½ cups)

½ cup chopped onion

1½ cups (8 ounces) diced cooked turkey breast

1 (10¾-ounce) can Healthy Request Cream of Mushroom Soup

½ cup + 1 tablespoon (2¼ ounces) shredded Kraft reduced-fat
    Cheddar cheese

2 cups skim milk

2 teaspoons dried parsley flakes

⅛ teaspoon black pepper

¼ cup (one 2-ounce jar) chopped pimiento, undrained

½ cup (one 2.5-ounce jar) sliced mushrooms, undrained

1 cup hot cooked spaghetti, rinsed and drained

In a large saucepan sprayed with butter-flavored cooking spray, sauté onion and turkey for 5 minutes. Stir in mushroom soup, Cheddar cheese, skim milk, parsley flakes, and black pepper. Add undrained pimiento, undrained mushrooms, and spaghetti. Mix well to combine. Lower heat and simmer for 12 to 15 minutes, stirring occasionally.

HINTS: 1. If you don't have leftovers, purchase a chunk of cooked turkey breast from your local deli.
      2. ¾ cup broken uncooked spaghetti usually cooks to about 1 cup.

Each serving equals:

HE: 2¾ Protein • ½ Skim Milk • ½ Bread •
½ Vegetable • ½ Slider • 1 Optional Calorie

283 Calories • 7 gm Fat • 29 gm Protein •
26 gm Carbohydrate • 575 mg Sodium •
326 mg Calcium • 2 gm Fiber

DIABETIC: 2½ Meat • 1 Starch • ½ Skim Milk

Turkey and Veggie Rice Soup ❄

Here's a wonderful way to use up those post–Turkey Day leftovers without eliciting groans of "Oh, no, not turkey again," from your family! Maybe it's the blend of rice and veggies, maybe it's the creamy texture of the soup itself, but this soup will produce only happy memories of the holiday's "big bird."

☻ Serves 4 (1½ cups)

2 cups (one 16-ounce can)
  Healthy Request
  Chicken Broth
2 cups water
½ cup chopped onion
¾ cup chopped celery
¾ cup shredded carrots
1½ cups (8 ounces) diced
  cooked turkey breast

1 teaspoon dried parsley
  flakes
⅛ teaspoon black pepper
1 (10¾-ounce) can Healthy
  Request Cream of
  Chicken Soup
⅔ cup (2 ounces) uncooked
  Minute Rice

In a large saucepan, combine chicken broth, water, onion, celery, and carrots. Bring mixture to a boil. Stir in turkey, parsley flakes, and black pepper. Lower heat, cover, and simmer for about 10 minutes or until vegetables are tender, stirring occasionally. Add chicken soup and uncooked rice. Mix well to combine. Re-cover and continue simmering for about 10 minutes or until rice is tender, stirring occasionally.

HINT: If you don't have leftovers, purchase a chunk of cooked turkey breast from your local deli.

Each serving equals:

HE: 2 Protein • 1 Vegetable • ½ Bread •
½ Slider • 13 Optional Calories

191 Calories • 3 gm Fat • 22 gm Protein • 19 gm
Carbohydrate • 610 mg Sodium •
31 mg Calcium • 1 gm Fiber

DIABETIC: 2 Meat • 1 Vegetable • 1 Starch

Meaty Soups and Chowders

D o you remember seeing ads for soup that was so jam-packed with chunks of potato and pieces of meat, you might be tempted to eat it with a fork instead of a spoon? Or the ones that offered a soup that "ate like a meal"? There are few things more irresistible than sitting down to a thick, hearty bowl of soup that's full of delicious meat and veggies. So full, in fact, that your spoon will almost stand straight up!

It's hard for me to believe sometimes how many years it's been since I sat on a stool in my mother's kitchen and watched her preparing soup in her great big old-fashioned soup kettle. She'd stand there, cutting up chunks of beef and potato, carrots and onions, and tossing them into the pot, while I got to stir the pot and inhale the incredible aroma that filled her kitchen. I can still close my eyes and recall how good her soup smelled, and of course how wonderful it tasted. Soup is a true comfort food, and no soup is more cozy and nourishing than rich, meaty blends stirred up with love.

Don't you just know you're going to be satisfied and happy when your first spoonful of soup contains lots of veggies (corn, tomatoes, celery, or peppers) and those tasty bites of beef or ham or frankfurters? You could please your family every night for days on end with the recipes in this section. Try my **Unstuffed Cabbage Soup** *when you all come home exhausted after a day of holiday shopping (it takes less than 30 minutes from start to finish). Invite a group of friends for a Halloween buffet while the kids are trick-or-treating, and serve* **Falling Leaves Soup***. And when you really, really need the kind of soothing only a hearty bowl of soup can provide, I offer* **Meaty Italian Corn Chowder** *to fill your tummy with creamy goodness!*

Meaty Soups
and Chowders

Farmers' Market Soup

There's something so beautiful and lush about all that fresh produce spread out before you at the farmers' market—don't you just want to take it all home? But what if you can't make it to the market but still want that tasty abundance in a kettle of soup? This recipe is a little bit of a "kitchen sink" of soups, with lots of different veggies stirred in. ☺ Serves 4 (1½ cups)

8 ounces ground 90% lean turkey or beef
½ cup chopped onion
1 cup fresh or frozen cut carrots, thawed
1 cup fresh or frozen cut green beans, thawed
½ cup chopped celery
1¾ cups (one 14½-ounce can) Swanson Beef Broth

1 (10¾-ounce) can Healthy Request Tomato Soup
1 teaspoon dried parsley flakes
¾ cup fresh or frozen peas
¾ cup fresh or frozen whole-kernel corn, thawed
1 cup chopped cabbage

In a large saucepan sprayed with butter-flavored cooking spray, brown meat. Stir in onion, carrots, green beans, celery, and beef broth. Bring mixture to a boil. Add tomato soup, parsley flakes, peas, corn, and cabbage. Mix well to combine. Lower heat, cover, and simmer for 15 minutes or until vegetables are tender, stirring occasionally.

HINT: Thaw carrots, green beans, and corn by placing in a colander and rinsing under hot water for one minute.

Each serving equals:

HE: 2 Vegetable • 1½ Protein • ¾ Bread • ½ Slider • 14 Optional Calories

218 Calories • 6 gm Fat • 15 gm Protein • 26 gm Carbohydrate • 678 mg Sodium • 53 mg Calcium • 5 gm Fiber

DIABETIC: 1½ Vegetable • 1½ Meat • 1 Starch

Falling Leaves Soup ❄

Are the trees in your yard already bare? Then you know it won't be long before snow covers the ground. It's definitely time for soup! This fast and flavorful mix tastes as if it's been bubbling away for hours instead of minutes. ☺ Serves 4 (1¼ cups)

> 8 ounces ground 90% lean turkey or beef
> ½ cup chopped onion
> ¾ cup chopped carrots
> ¾ cup chopped celery
> 1 cup (5 ounces) diced raw potatoes
> 1¾ cups (one 15-ounce can) Swanson Beef Broth
> 2 cups (one 16-ounce can) tomatoes, coarsely chopped and
>   undrained
> 1 teaspoon pourable Sugar Twin
> 1 teaspoon dried basil
> ¼ teaspoon black pepper

In a large saucepan sprayed with butter-flavored cooking spray, brown meat. Stir in onion, carrots, celery, potatoes, and beef broth. Bring mixture to a boil. Add undrained tomatoes, Sugar Twin, basil, and black pepper. Mix well to combine. Lower heat, cover, and simmer for about 15 to 20 minutes or until vegetables are tender, stirring occasionally.

Each serving equals:

HE: 2 Vegetable • 1½ Protein • ¼ Bread •
9 Optional Calories

153 Calories • 5 gm Fat • 13 gm Protein •
14 gm Carbohydrate • 449 mg Sodium •
34 mg Calcium • 3 gm Fiber

DIABETIC: 2 Vegetable • 1½ Meat • ½ Starch

Meaty Italian Corn Chowder ❄

Ever have one of those nights when you just can't decide what to make for dinner—something Italian or an all-American favorite? I must have been experiencing one of those days when this recipe emerged from my brain! It's really a blend of down-home flavors spiced up with a little Roman pizzazz!

◑ Serves 4 (1 cup)

> 8 ounces ground 90% lean turkey or beef
> ½ cup chopped onion
> 1 cup (5 ounces) diced raw potatoes
> 1¾ cups water ☆
> 1 cup (one 8-ounce can) cream-style corn
> ½ cup frozen whole-kernel corn, thawed
> ¼ teaspoon dried minced garlic
> 1 teaspoon Italian seasoning
> ⅔ cup Carnation Nonfat Dry Milk Powder
> ¼ cup (¾ ounce) grated Kraft fat-free Parmesan cheese

In a medium saucepan sprayed with olive oil–flavored cooking spray, brown meat. Add onion, potatoes, and 1 cup water. Mix well to combine. Bring mixture to a boil. Stir in cream-style corn, whole-kernel corn, garlic, and Italian seasoning. In a small bowl, combine remaining ¾ cup water and dry milk powder. Add milk mixture to corn mixture. Mix well to combine. Lower heat and simmer for 10 minutes or until mixture is heated through, stirring occasionally. When serving, sprinkle 1 tablespoon Parmesan cheese over top of each bowl.

HINT: Thaw corn by placing in a colander and rinsing under hot water for one minute.

Each serving equals:

HE: 1¾ Protein • 1 Bread • ½ Skim Milk •
¼ Vegetable

245 Calories • 5 gm Fat • 17 gm Protein •
33 gm Carbohydrate • 522 mg Sodium •
148 mg Calcium • 3 gm Fiber

DIABETIC: 2 Meat • 1½ Starch • ½ Skim Milk

Unstuffed Cabbage Soup

Stuffed cabbage is one of the most popular recipes in all Eastern European cuisines, including that of my Bohemian ancestors. I thought, hmm, why not whisk that wonderful flavor into a fragrant pot of tummy-warming soup? The result was more delicious than I dreamed it would be!   ☻   Serves 4 (1½ cups)

8 ounces ground 90% lean turkey or beef
½ cup chopped onion
1 (10¾-ounce) can Healthy Request Tomato Soup
1¾ cups (one 15-ounce can) Hunt's Tomato Sauce
2 cups water
1 teaspoon dried parsley flakes
½ teaspoon Worcestershire sauce
⅛ teaspoon black pepper
2 cups shredded cabbage
⅔ cup (2 ounces) uncooked Minute Rice

In a large saucepan sprayed with butter-flavored cooking spray, brown meat and onion. Stir in tomato soup, tomato sauce, water, parsley flakes, Worcestershire sauce, and black pepper. Bring mixture to a boil. Add cabbage and uncooked rice. Mix well to combine. Lower heat, cover, and simmer for about 15 minutes or until cabbage and rice are tender, stirring occasionally.

Each serving equals:

HE: 3 Vegetable • 1½ Protein • ½ Bread • ½ Slider • 5 Optional Calories

202 Calories • 6 gm Fat • 13 gm Protein • 24 gm Carbohydrate • 898 mg Sodium • 33 mg Calcium • 4 gm Fiber

DIABETIC: 2 Vegetable • 1½ Meat • 1 Starch

Pam's Quick Pastafazool ❄

My daughter-in-law Pam doesn't let her husband, James, do all the cooking at their house, even though she now has three wonderful little boys to care for. This recipe is one of her favorites because it mingles pasta and beans with spicy meat and tomato sauce for a truly yummy, family-pleasing meal.

☻ Serves 4 (1¼ cups)

> 8 ounces ground 90% lean turkey or beef
> 6 ounces (one 8-ounce can) red kidney beans, rinsed and drained
> 1 cup (one 8-ounce can) Hunt's Tomato Sauce
> 1¾ cups (one 15-ounce can) Swanson Beef Broth
> ¾ cup water
> 1½ cups cooked elbow macaroni, rinsed and drained
> 1 tablespoon chili seasoning
> 1 tablespoon Italian seasoning
> ¼ cup (¾ ounce) grated Kraft fat-free Parmesan cheese

In a large saucepan sprayed with olive oil–flavored cooking spray, brown meat. Stir in kidney beans, tomato sauce, beef broth, and water. Bring mixture to a boil. Add macaroni, chili seasoning, and Italian seasoning. Mix well to combine. Lower heat, cover, and simmer for 15 minutes, stirring occasionally. When serving, sprinkle 1 tablespoon Parmesan cheese over top of each bowl.

HINT: 1 cup of uncooked macaroni usually cooks to about 1½ cups.

Each serving equals:

HE: 2½ Protein • 1 Vegetable • ¾ Bread •
8 Optional Calories

---

221 Calories • 5 gm Fat • 17 gm Protein •
27 gm Carbohydrate • 848 mg Sodium •
29 mg Calcium • 5 gm Fiber

DIABETIC: 1½ Meat • 1 Starch • 1 Vegetable

Cliff's Taco Soup

If Cliff had his way, we'd stop for Mexican food every night as we tour the nation. I once asked if he had put a special "Mexican restaurant radar tracker" in the motorhome, so often did it seem that we pulled up beside one! It's a good thing I enjoy the tangy flavors almost as much as he does. ☻ Serves 4 (1¼ cups)

> 8 ounces ground 90% lean turkey or beef
> ½ cup chopped onion
> 1 cup (one 8-ounce can) Hunt's Tomato Sauce
> 1¾ cups water
> 2 teaspoons taco seasoning
> ⅛ teaspoon black pepper
> 6 ounces (one 8-ounce can) red kidney beans, rinsed and drained
> 1 cup frozen whole-kernel corn
> ⅓ cup (1½ ounces) shredded Kraft reduced-fat Cheddar cheese
> ½ cup (¾ ounce) crushed Frito-Lay reduced-fat corn chips
> ¼ cup Land O Lakes no-fat sour cream

In a large saucepan sprayed with butter-flavored cooking spray, brown meat and onion. Stir in tomato sauce, water, taco seasoning, and black pepper. Bring mixture to a boil. Add kidney beans and corn. Mix well to combine. Lower heat and simmer for 10 to 15 minutes, stirring occasionally. When serving, top each bowl with 1½ tablespoons Cheddar cheese, 2 tablespoons corn chips, and 1 tablespoon sour cream.

Each serving equals:

HE: 2¾ Protein • 1¼ Vegetable • ¾ Bread •
15 Optional Calories

243 Calories • 7 gm Fat • 18 gm Protein •
27 gm Carbohydrate • 625 mg Sodium •
120 mg Calcium • 6 gm Fiber

DIABETIC: 2½ Meat • 1 Vegetable • 1 Starch

Rustic Pizza Soup

You can tell a lot about a recipe by how the kitchen staff at Healthy Exchanges reacts while we're testing it. This soup smelled so outrageously good, I think nearly everyone asked for a sample—and that means a lot to me! If you love pizza (doesn't everyone?) then this will soon be one of your "regulars"!   ☻   Serves 4

8 ounces ground 90% lean turkey or beef
½ cup chopped onion
½ cup (one 2.5-ounce jar) sliced mushrooms, undrained
1 (10¾-ounce) can Healthy Request Tomato Soup
2 cups Healthy Request tomato juice or any reduced-sodium
     tomato juice
1½ teaspoons pizza or Italian seasoning
⅓ cup (1½ ounces) shredded Kraft reduced-fat Cheddar cheese
¼ cup (¾ ounce) grated Kraft fat-free Parmesan cheese
4 slices reduced-calorie Italian bread, toasted and cubed

In a large saucepan sprayed with butter-flavored cooking spray, brown meat and onion. Stir in undrained mushrooms, tomato soup, tomato juice, and pizza seasoning. Add Cheddar cheese and Parmesan cheese. Mix well to combine. Lower heat and simmer for 6 to 8 minutes or until mixture is heated through and cheeses melt. For each serving, place ¼ of the bread cubes in a bowl and spoon about 1 cup of hot soup over top. Serve at once.

Each serving equals:

HE: 2¼ Protein • 1½ Vegetable • ½ Bread •
½ Slider • 5 Optional Calories

244 Calories • 8 gm Fat • 18 gm Protein •
25 gm Carbohydrate • 663 mg Sodium •
113 mg Calcium • 5 gm Fiber

DIABETIC: 2 Meat • 1 Vegetable •
1 Starch/Carbohydrate

Cheeseburger Rice Soup

I could have called this "Fast-Food Soup," because I bet cheese-burgers are the favorite fast-food choice of Americans from coast to coast! (My son Tommy would agree!) This utterly satisfying and family-pleasing dish is great for a buffet at a teenagers' party, but you don't need a special occasion to stir it up.

Serves 6 (1⅓ cups)

> 8 ounces ground 90% lean turkey or beef
> ½ cup shredded carrots
> ½ cup finely chopped celery
> ½ cup finely chopped onion
> 2 cups (one 16-ounce can) Healthy Request Chicken Broth
> 1 cup water
> 1½ cups hot cooked rice
> ¾ cup (3 ounces) shredded Kraft reduced-fat Cheddar cheese
> 1 teaspoon dried parsley flakes
> 1 (10¾-ounce) can Healthy Request Cream of Mushroom Soup
> 1½ cups (one 12-fluid-ounce can) Carnation Evaporated Skim
>   Milk
> ¼ cup Land O Lakes no-fat sour cream

In a large saucepan sprayed with butter-flavored cooking spray, brown meat. Add carrots, celery, onion, chicken broth, and water. Mix well to combine. Bring mixture to a boil. Lower heat, cover, and simmer for 10 minutes or until vegetables are tender. Stir in rice, Cheddar cheese, and parsley flakes. Add mushroom soup and evaporated skim milk. Mix well to combine. Continue simmering for 10 minutes or until mixture is heated through and cheese melts, stirring occasionally. Just before serving, fold in sour cream.

HINT: 1 cup uncooked rice usually cooks to about 1½ cups.

Each serving equals:

HE: 1⅔ Protein • ½ Skim Milk • ½ Bread •
½ Vegetable • ½ Slider • 3 Optional Calories

226 Calories • 6 gm Fat • 18 gm Protein •
25 gm Carbohydrate • 614 mg Sodium •
336 mg Calcium • 1 gm Fiber

DIABETIC: 1½ Meat • 1 Starch/Carbohydrate •
½ Skim Milk

Skillet Beef Stew

Traditional beef stew used to require hours on the stove before you could serve it, but I think you'll be pleased to taste just how rich the flavors are in this substantially speedier version! The broth and flour perform a little "thickening magic" in seconds, and you've got a skillet supper that really satisfies. ☻ Serves 4 (1 cup)

> 8 ounces ground 90% lean turkey or beef
> ½ cup sliced onion
> 1¾ cups (one 14½-ounce can) Swanson Beef Broth
> 3 tablespoons all-purpose flour
> ⅛ teaspoon black pepper
> 1½ cups thinly sliced carrots
> 1 cup thinly sliced celery

In a large skillet sprayed with butter-flavored cooking spray, brown meat and onion. In a covered jar, combine beef broth, flour, and black pepper. Shake well to blend. Pour broth mixture over meat. Stir in carrots and celery. Lower heat, cover, and simmer for 25 minutes or until vegetables are tender, stirring occasionally.

Each serving equals:

> HE: 1½ Protein • 1½ Vegetable • ¼ Bread •
> 9 Optional Calories
>
> ---
> 133 Calories • 5 gm Fat • 12 gm Protein •
> 10 gm Carbohydrate • 462 mg Sodium •
> 31 mg Calcium • 2 gm Fiber
> ---
> DIABETIC: 1½ Meat • 1 Vegetable

Stroganoff Stew

Does it surprise you to learn that you can use fat-free sour cream to make a truly scrumptious hot dish like this one? It's a good-for-you dairy product that doesn't fall apart when you cook with it. Instead, it adds a luscious, creamy texture to a beloved meaty classic!

Serves 4 (1½ cups)

8 ounces ground 90% lean turkey or beef
1 cup finely chopped celery
½ cup (one 2.5-ounce jar) sliced mushrooms, undrained
1 (10¾-ounce) can Healthy Request Cream of Mushroom Soup
½ cup Land O Lakes no-fat sour cream
2 cups skim milk
1 cup hot cooked noodles, rinsed and drained
1 teaspoon dried onion flakes
1 teaspoon dried parsley flakes
⅛ teaspoon black pepper

In a large saucepan sprayed with butter-flavored cooking spray, brown meat and celery. Stir in undrained mushrooms, mushroom soup, sour cream, and skim milk. Add noodles, onion flakes, parsley flakes, and black pepper. Mix well to combine. Lower heat and simmer for 10 minutes, stirring occasionally.

HINT: A scant 1 cup uncooked noodles usually cooks to about 1 cup.

Each serving equals:

HE: 1½ Protein • ¾ Vegetable • ½ Skim Milk •
½ Bread • ¾ Slider • 11 Optional Calories

255 Calories • 7 gm Fat • 18 gm Protein •
30 gm Carbohydrate • 569 mg Sodium •
254 mg Calcium • 2 gm Fiber

DIABETIC: 1½ Meat • 1½ Starch/Carbohydrate •
½ Vegetable • ½ Skim Milk

Creamy Meatball Stew with Dumplings

I've always liked nibbling on tiny meatballs, ever since I was a child. Back then, it was fun to imagine being invited to an adult party where they were served on toothpicks as hors d'oeuvres. Now, I get to invite anyone I want to share in the party featuring this delectable soup! ☻ Serves 6

16 ounces ground 90% lean turkey or beef
½ cup finely chopped onion
¾ cup Land O Lakes no-fat sour cream ☆
1 cup + 2 tablespoons Bisquick Reduced Fat Baking Mix ☆
2 teaspoons dried parsley flakes
1 (10¾-ounce) can Healthy Request Cream of Celery Soup
½ cup + 2 tablespoons skim milk ☆
2 cups (one 16-ounce can) cut green beans, rinsed and drained
2 cups (one 16-ounce can) cut carrots, rinsed and drained

In a large bowl, combine meat, onion, ¼ cup sour cream, 2 tablespoons baking mix, and parsley flakes. Form mixture into 30 (1-inch) meatballs. Arrange meatballs in a large skillet sprayed with butter-flavored cooking spray. Brown meatballs for 2 to 3 minutes on each side. In a large bowl, combine celery soup, ¼ cup sour cream, and ½ cup skim milk. Stir in green beans and carrots. Spoon vegetable mixture evenly over meatballs. Bring mixture to a boil, stirring occasionally, and being careful not to break meatballs. Meanwhile, in a small bowl, combine remaining 1 cup baking mix, remaining ¼ cup sour cream, and remaining 2 tablespoons skim milk. Drop batter by tablespoonful into hot mixture to form 6 dumplings. Lower heat and simmer for 10 minutes. Cover and continue simmering for 15 to 20 minutes or until dumplings are firm. For each serving, place 1 dumpling and 5 meatballs in a bowl and evenly spoon stew over top.

Each serving equals:

HE: 2 Protein • 1½ Vegetable • 1 Bread •
¾ Slider • 6 Optional Calories

---

281 Calories • 9 gm Fat • 18 gm Protein •
32 gm Carbohydrate • 605 mg Sodium •
136 mg Calcium • 2 gm Fiber

DIABETIC: 2 Meat • 1½ Starch/Carbohydrate •
1 Vegetable

Mexican Stew

I really enjoy experimenting with different spice combinations as part of creating new recipes. That's probably why I'm so proud of my line of JO's Spices, which add extra pleasure to already yummy dishes. Here, I think you'll agree that the blend of garlic, chili seasoning, and just a bit of Worcestershire sauce turn ordinary ingredients into something really extraordinary!

☻ Serves 4 (¾ cup)

> 2 cups (10 ounces) diced lean cooked roast beef
> ¾ cup chopped onion
> ¾ cup chopped green bell pepper
> ¼ cup finely chopped celery
> 1¾ cups (one 14½-ounce can) stewed tomatoes, coarsely chopped
>   and undrained
> ½ teaspoon dried minced garlic
> 1 teaspoon Worcestershire sauce
> 2 teaspoons chili seasoning

In a large skillet sprayed with olive oil–flavored cooking spray, sauté roast beef, onion, green pepper, and celery for 10 minutes. Stir in undrained tomatoes, garlic, Worcestershire sauce, and chili seasoning. Lower heat and simmer for 10 minutes or until vegetables are tender, stirring often.

HINTS: 1. If you don't have leftovers, purchase a chunk of lean cooked roast beef from your local deli or use Healthy Choice Deli slices.
2. Good served over pasta, rice, potatoes, or cornbread.

Each serving equals:

HE: 2½ Protein • 1¾ Vegetable

173 Calories • 5 gm Fat • 22 gm Protein •
10 gm Carbohydrate • 383 mg Sodium •
72 mg Calcium • 2 gm Fiber

DIABETIC: 2½ Meat • 1½ Vegetable

Italian Beef Noodle Soup

This is just the kind of recipe that "works" for a working mom who'd rather spend time with her family than hours in the kitchen after a long day on the job! Most of the ingredients are on your pantry shelf, and you can always pick up the meat you need on the way home. What a cozy, comforting dish to share with those you love! ☻ Serves 4 (1¼ cups)

> 1½ cups (8 ounces) diced lean cooked roast beef
> ¼ cup chopped onion
> 1¾ cups (one 15-ounce can) Swanson Beef Broth
> 1¾ cups (one 14½-ounce can) stewed tomatoes, undrained
> 1 cup water
> 1½ teaspoons Italian seasoning
> 1 teaspoon pourable Sugar Twin
> ⅛ teaspoon black pepper
> 1¾ cups (3 ounces) uncooked fine egg noodles

In a medium saucepan sprayed with olive oil–flavored cooking spray, brown beef and onion for 5 minutes. Add beef broth, undrained tomatoes, water, Italian seasoning, Sugar Twin, and black pepper. Mix well to combine. Bring mixture to a boil. Stir in uncooked noodles. Lower heat and simmer for 20 to 25 minutes, stirring occasionally.

HINT: If you don't have leftovers, purchase a chunk of lean cooked roast beef from your local deli or use Healthy Choice Deli slices.

Each serving equals:

HE: 2 Protein • 1 Bread • 1 Vegetable •
9 Optional Calories

---

293 Calories • 5 gm Fat • 24 gm Protein •
38 gm Carbohydrate • 714 mg Sodium •
68 mg Calcium • 2 gm Fiber

DIABETIC: 2 Meat • 1½ Starch • 1 Vegetable

Beef and Barley Soup

A friend once told me that she'd never made a barley soup from scratch, and she had no idea how much to add to her bubbling kettle of broth. When she tossed in a cupful, she was astonished to discover that all the liquid quickly vanished, and she had a potful of barley, and almost no soup! You'll be glad to know I've done the measuring for you—and here, just a few tablespoons is enough to serve six.   ❂   Serves 6 (1½ cups)

> 1¾ cups (one 14½-ounce can) Swanson Beef Broth
> 1 cup water
> 1 teaspoon dried parsley flakes
> 2 cups (one 16-ounce can) tomatoes, coarsely chopped and
>   undrained
> 1½ cups (8 ounces) diced lean cooked roast beef
> ½ cup finely diced celery
> ½ cup chopped onion
> ½ cup diced carrots
> 2 cups shredded cabbage
> 1 cup (5 ounces) finely diced raw potatoes
> ½ cup frozen green beans
> 3 tablespoons (¾ ounce) barley
> ¼ teaspoon black pepper

In a slow cooker container, combine beef broth, water, parsley flakes, and undrained tomatoes. Add roast beef, celery, onion, carrots, cabbage, potatoes, green beans, barley, and black pepper. Mix well to combine. Cover and cook on LOW for 8 to 10 hours. Stir well before serving.

HINT: If you don't have leftovers, purchase a chunk of lean cooked roast beef from your local deli or use Healthy Choice Deli slices.

Each serving equals:

HE: 2 Vegetable • 1⅓ Protein • ⅓ Bread •
6 Optional Calories

139 Calories • 3 gm Fat • 14 gm Protein •
14 gm Carbohydrate • 438 mg Sodium •
50 mg Calcium • 2 gm Fiber

DIABETIC: 1½ Vegetable • 1 Meat • ½ Starch

Chunky Vegetable Beef Soup ❄

Not everyone loves chopping vegetables as much as I do (I find it surprisingly soothing!), but that's probably why all those "kitchen helper" appliances do so well. This is a great recipe to try with your new salad maker or food processor, but it's also easily made with pre-chopped and pre-shredded veggies straight from the market.

◐ Serves 4 (1¼ cups)

> 1¾ cups (one 15-ounce can) Swanson Beef Broth
> ½ cup chopped onion
> ¾ cup shredded carrots
> ¾ cup chopped celery
> 1 cup (one 8-ounce can) Hunt's Tomato Sauce
> ¾ cup water
> 1 cup (5 ounces) diced lean cooked roast beef
> 2 cups shredded cabbage
> 1 teaspoon dried parsley flakes
> ¼ teaspoon black pepper

In a large saucepan, combine beef broth, onion, carrots, and celery. Bring mixture to a boil. Stir in tomato sauce, water, and roast beef. Add cabbage, parsley flakes, and black pepper. Mix well to combine. Lower heat and simmer for about 20 to 25 minutes or until vegetables are tender, stirring occasionally.

HINT: If you don't have leftovers, purchase a chunk of lean cooked roast beef from your local deli or use Healthy Choice Deli slices.

Each serving equals:

HE: 3 Vegetable • 1¼ Protein • 9 Optional Calories

131 Calories • 3 gm Fat • 13 gm Protein •
13 gm Carbohydrate • 806 mg Sodium •
54 mg Calcium • 3 gm Fiber

DIABETIC: 2½ Vegetable • 1 Meat

Grande Beef and Cabbage Soup ❄

This protein-rich dish takes very little watching, so once you've mixed the ingredients and set the pot to simmer, you're free to catch up on the evening news, return a few phone calls, or just flip through a favorite magazine. What a lot of hearty flavor for very few calories and almost no fat! ◐ Serves 4 (1½ cups)

1¾ cups (one 15-ounce can) Swanson Beef Broth
1 cup (one 8-ounce can) stewed tomatoes, coarsely chopped and undrained
1 cup water
1 cup (5 ounces) diced lean cooked roast beef
½ cup chopped onion
1½ teaspoons chili seasoning
1 teaspoon dried parsley flakes
2½ cups chopped cabbage
6 ounces (one 8-ounce can) red kidney beans, rinsed and drained

In a large saucepan, combine beef broth, undrained tomatoes, and water. Bring mixture to a boil. Stir in roast beef, onion, chili seasoning, and parsley flakes. Add cabbage and kidney beans. Mix well to combine. Lower heat, cover, and simmer for about 20 to 25 minutes or until vegetables are tender, stirring occasionally.

HINT: If you don't have leftovers, purchase a chunk of lean cooked roast beef from your local deli or use Healthy Choice Deli slices.

Each serving equals:

HE: 2 Protein • 2 Vegetable • 9 Optional Calories

139 Calories • 3 gm Fat • 14 gm Protein •
14 gm Carbohydrate • 572 mg Sodium •
70 mg Calcium • 4 gm Fiber

DIABETIC: 2 Meat • 1 Vegetable • ½ Starch

Tex-Mex Pepperpot Soup

Here's a dish that takes great advantage of the tasty fat-free gravies now available across the nation! I always make sure to keep some on the shelf alongside my cans of stewed tomatoes and various healthy soups. This mix of tangy flavors in one bowl is perfect for those crisp fall days when your appetite is all revved up.

● Serves 4 (1¼ cups)

> 1¾ cups (one 15-ounce can) Swanson Beef Broth
> 1½ cups (8 ounces) diced lean cooked roast beef
> 1 cup frozen whole-kernel corn, thawed
> 1 cup (one 8-ounce can) stewed tomatoes, coarsely chopped and
>   undrained
> ½ cup finely chopped onion
> ½ cup chopped green bell pepper
> ¼ cup (one 2-ounce jar) chopped pimiento, undrained
> 1 teaspoon dried parsley flakes
> 1 (12-ounce) jar Heinz Fat Free Beef Gravy

In a large saucepan, combine beef broth, roast beef, corn, and undrained stewed tomatoes. Bring mixture to a boil. Add onion, green pepper, undrained pimiento, and parsley flakes. Mix well to combine. Lower heat, cover, and simmer for 15 minutes. Stir in gravy. Continue simmering 5 minutes or until mixture is heated through and vegetables are tender, stirring occasionally.

HINTS: 1. If you don't have leftovers, purchase a chunk of lean cooked roast beef from your local deli or use Healthy Choice Deli slices.
        2. Thaw corn by placing in a colander and rinsing under hot water for one minute.

Each serving equals:

HE: 2 Protein • 1 Vegetable • ½ Bread •
½ Slider • 6 Optional Calories

205 Calories • 5 gm Fat • 20 gm Protein •
20 gm Carbohydrate • 989 mg Sodium •
42 mg Calcium • 2 gm Fiber

DIABETIC: 2 Meat • 1 Vegetable • 1 Starch

Pork, Potato, and Kraut Stew

I remember putting these few ingredients into the slow cooker on a day when we had so much to do, we didn't get home for dinner until hours later. When I lifted the cover, I beckoned to Cliff and said, "If this isn't the kind of aroma that'll keep marriages together, I don't know what is!" He laughed, and held out his plate.

☻ Serves 4 (1½ cups)

> *16 ounces lean pork tenderloins or cutlets, cut into 20 pieces*
> *1 cup chopped onion*
> *2 cups (one 16-ounce can) sauerkraut, well drained*
> *3 cups (15 ounces) chopped raw potatoes*
> *1 (10¾-ounce) can Healthy Request Cream of Mushroom Soup*

In a slow cooker container, combine meat, onion, sauerkraut, and potatoes. Stir in mushroom soup. Cover and cook on LOW for 6 to 8 hours. Stir well just before serving.

Each serving equals:

HE: 3 Protein • 1½ Vegetable • ¾ Bread •

½ Slider • 1 Optional Calorie

304 Calories • 8 gm Fat • 29 gm Protein •
29 gm Carbohydrate • 960 mg Sodium •
124 mg Calcium • 5 gm Fiber

DIABETIC: 3 Meat • 1½ Vegetable • 1½ Starch

Tom's Macaroni and Cheese with Ham Soup

Pleasing the taste buds of your children is a great goal for a home cook, and you'll always have a head start if you consider the foods they like best. My son Tommy, now married and living in Arizona, still craves macaroni and cheese whenever he can get it, so I created this tasty soup for him.　❂　Serves 6 (1 full cup)

> 1 (10¾-ounce) can Healthy Request Cream of Mushroom Soup
> 3 cups skim milk
> 1½ cups (6 ounces) shredded Kraft reduced-fat Cheddar cheese
> 2 teaspoons prepared mustard
> 1 teaspoon dried parsley flakes
> ⅛ teaspoon black pepper
> 1½ cups hot cooked elbow macaroni, rinsed and drained
> 1 full cup (6 ounces) diced Dubuque 97% fat-free ham or any
>   extra-lean ham

In a large saucepan, combine mushroom soup and skim milk. Stir in Cheddar cheese, mustard, parsley flakes, and black pepper. Add macaroni and ham. Mix well to combine. Cook over medium-low heat for 10 minutes or until mixture is heated through and cheese melts, stirring occasionally.

HINT:　1 cup uncooked elbow macaroni usually cooks to about 1½ cups.

Each serving equals:

> HE: 2 Protein • ½ Bread • ½ Skim Milk • ¼ Slider • 8 Optional Calories
>
> ---
>
> 223 Calories • 7 gm Fat • 18 gm Protein • 22 gm Carbohydrate • 763 mg Sodium • 376 mg Calcium • 1 gm Fiber
>
> ---
>
> DIABETIC: 1½ Meat • 1 Starch • ½ Skim Milk

Chunky Pea Soup with Ham-and-Cheese Dumplings

Blenders are a great tool for making thick and rich soups that are low in fat but high in flavor! You can thicken just about any soup by spooning some of the cooked vegetables into your blender and letting it run for 10 or 20 seconds, then pouring the mixture back into the saucepan. I think these ham-and-cheese dumplings are among the tastiest I've ever created—let me know if you agree!

☻ Serves 6 (1 cup soup and 1 dumpling)

> 1 cup (one 8-ounce can) small peas, rinsed and drained
> 2 cups water ☆
> 2 cups (one 16-ounce can) Healthy Request Chicken Broth
> 1/8 teaspoon black pepper
> 1 cup (5 ounces) diced raw potatoes
> 1/2 cup frozen peas
> 3/4 cup shredded carrots
> 1/4 cup finely chopped onion
> 1/2 cup (3 ounces) finely diced Dubuque 97% fat-free ham or any
>   extra-lean ham
> 6 tablespoons Bisquick Reduced Fat Baking Mix
> 1 teaspoon dried parsley flakes
> 1/4 cup skim milk
> 3 tablespoons (3/4 ounce) shredded Kraft reduced-fat Cheddar
>   cheese

In a blender container, combine canned peas and 1/2 cup water. Cover and process on PUREE for 30 seconds or until mixture is smooth. In a large saucepan, combine pea puree, remaining 1 1/2 cups water, chicken broth, and black pepper. Add potatoes, frozen peas, carrots, and onion. Mix well to combine. Bring mixture to a boil. Lower heat, cover, and simmer for 15 minutes. In a medium bowl, combine ham, baking mix, and parsley flakes. Add skim milk and Cheddar cheese. Mix gently to combine. Drop batter by tablespoonful into hot mixture to form 6 dumplings. Cover and continue simmering for 10 to 12 minutes or until dumplings are firm.

Each serving equals:

HE: 1 Bread • ½ Protein • ⅓ Vegetable • ¼ Slider • 9 Optional Calories

148 Calories • 4 gm Fat • 11 gm Protein • 18 gm Carbohydrate • 510 mg Sodium • 140 mg Calcium • 4 gm Fiber

DIABETIC: 1½ Starch • ½ Meat

Home Style Ham Stew ❄

Here's a festive mix of frozen veggies, combined for a colorful and flavorful stick-to-your-ribs meal! Did you know that frozen veggies may be among the healthiest we eat, because they're picked at perfect ripeness and flash-frozen to stay that way until you use them? If they don't come to the table right from your garden, then frozen veggies may be the next best thing! ☺ Serves 4 (1 cup)

2 cups (one 16-ounce can) tomatoes, chopped and undrained
1 cup frozen peas, thawed
1 cup frozen whole-kernel corn, thawed
1 cup frozen cut green beans, thawed
1 cup frozen sliced carrots, thawed
½ cup chopped onion
1 full cup (6 ounces) diced Dubuque 97% fat-free ham or any
    extra-lean ham
2 teaspoons dried parsley flakes
⅛ teaspoon black pepper

In a large skillet, combine undrained tomatoes, peas, corn, green beans, and carrots. Add onions, ham, parsley flakes, and black pepper. Mix well to combine. Bring mixture to a boil. Lower heat, cover, and simmer for 15 to 20 minutes or until vegetables are tender, stirring occasionally.

HINT: Thaw vegetables by placing in a colander and rinsing under hot water for one minute.

Each serving equals:

HE: 2¼ Vegetable • 1 Bread • 1 Protein

162 Calories • 2 gm Fat • 11 gm Protein •
25 gm Carbohydrate • 576 mg Sodium •
61 mg Calcium • 5 gm Fiber

DIABETIC: 2 Vegetable • 1 Starch • 1 Meat

Mom's Ham and Cabbage Soup ❄

When I was a little girl, I used to take my mother's ham and cabbage soup for granted. It was my dad's favorite, and she fixed it to please him. To me, it was just soup. Now, though, it's special to me because it takes me back to those happy days. I think the recipes of our childhood become ever more cherished as we grow older. Why not make some new memories with this wholesome and appetizing soup?　　❂　　Serves 4 (1⅓ cups)

> 3 cups hot water
> 1½ cups thinly sliced carrots
> 1 cup (5 ounces) diced raw potatoes
> ½ cup chopped onion
> 1½ full cups (9 ounces) diced Dubuque 97% fat-free ham or any
> 　　extra-lean ham
> 3 cups shredded cabbage
> 1 teaspoon dried parsley flakes
> ¼ teaspoon black pepper

In a large saucepan, combine water, carrots, potatoes, and onion. Bring mixture to a boil. Stir in ham, cabbage, parsley flakes, and black pepper. Lower heat, cover, and simmer for about 20 to 25 minutes or until vegetables are tender, stirring occasionally.

Each serving equals:

HE: 2½ Vegetable • 1½ Protein • ¼ Bread

---

118 Calories • 2 gm Fat • 12 gm Protein •
13 gm Carbohydrate • 575 mg Sodium •
47 mg Calcium • 3 gm Fiber

DIABETIC: 2 Vegetable • 1½ Meat • ½ Starch

Cauliflower-Ham Chowder   ❄

What a man-pleasing recipe this hearty dish is, made even thicker and richer when you puree some of the cooked vegetables to add to the kettle! (It's also beloved by my daughter Becky!) Don't you just love the idea of ham and cheese, America's most favorite sandwich combo, stirred into a tasty chowder?

❂ Serves 4 (1¼ cups)

> 3 cups frozen chopped cauliflower, thawed
> 2 cups (one 16-ounce can) Healthy Request Chicken Broth
> ½ cup chopped onion
> 1 cup diced celery
> 1½ cups (one 12-fluid-ounce can) Carnation Evaporated Skim Milk
> 3 tablespoons all-purpose flour
> 1½ cups (9 ounces) diced Dubuque 97% fat-free ham or any extra-lean ham
> ¾ cup (3 ounces) shredded Kraft reduced-fat Cheddar cheese

In a large saucepan, combine cauliflower, chicken broth, onion, and celery. Bring mixture to a boil. Lower heat, cover, and simmer for 20 to 25 minutes or until vegetables are tender, stirring occasionally. Pour 1½ cups of hot mixture into a blender container. Cover and process on HIGH for 15 to 20 seconds or until mixture is smooth. Pour blended mixture back into saucepan. In a covered jar, combine evaporated skim milk and flour. Shake well to blend. Add milk mixture to cauliflower mixture. Mix well to combine. Stir in ham and Cheddar cheese. Lower heat and simmer for about 10 minutes or until mixture is heated through and cheese melts, stirring occasionally.

HINT: Thaw cauliflower by placing in a colander and rinsing under hot water for one minute.

Each serving equals:

HE: 2½ Protein • 2¼ Vegetable • ¾ Skim Milk • ¼ Bread • 8 Optional Calories

258 Calories • 6 gm Fat • 27 gm Protein • 24 gm Carbohydrate • 1118 mg Sodium • 451 mg Calcium • 2 gm Fiber

DIABETIC: 2½ Meat • 2 Vegetable • 1 Skim Milk

Ham-Tomato Chowder

A salad and a roll may be all you need with this filling soup.

○ Serves 4 (1½ cups)

> 2 cups (one 16-ounce can) Healthy Request Chicken Broth
> 1¾ cups (one 14½-ounce can) stewed tomatoes, coarsely chopped
> and undrained
> ½ cup chopped celery
> ¼ cup finely chopped onion
> 1 cup frozen whole-kernel corn, thawed
> ½ cup frozen peas, thawed
> 1⅓ cups skim milk
> 3 tablespoons all-purpose flour
> 2 teaspoons dried parsley flakes
> ⅛ teaspoon black pepper
> 1 full cup (6 ounces) diced Dubuque 97% fat-free ham or any
> extra-lean ham
> ¾ cup (3 ounces) shredded Kraft reduced-fat Cheddar cheese

In a large saucepan, combine chicken broth, undrained tomatoes, celery, and onion. Bring mixture to a boil. Stir in corn and peas. Lower heat, cover, and simmer for 30 minutes or until vegetables are tender, stirring occasionally. In a covered jar, combine skim milk, flour, parsley flakes, and black pepper. Shake well to blend. Add milk mixture to broth mixture. Mix well to combine. Stir in ham and Cheddar cheese. Continue simmering for 5 minutes or until mixture thickens and cheese melts, stirring often.

HINT: Thaw corn and peas by placing in a colander and rinsing under hot water for one minute.

Each serving equals:

HE: 2 Protein • 1¼ Vegetable • 1 Bread •
⅓ Skim Milk • 8 Optional Calories

245 Calories • 5 gm Fat • 20 gm Protein •
30 gm Carbohydrate • 952 mg Sodium •
307 mg Calcium • 3 gm Fiber

DIABETIC: 2 Meat • 1 Vegetable • 1 Starch •
½ Skim Milk

Creamed Chipped Beef and Cabbage Chowder

❄

This recipe takes a traditional '50s-style supper dish and transforms it into a soup that's delightfully rich and oh-so-filling! If you've never enjoyed the original version of this "retro" classic, give this recipe a try! ☻ Serves 4 (1½ cups)

1 cup chopped onion
1 cup thinly sliced celery
2 cups (10 ounces) diced raw potatoes
2 cups coarsely chopped cabbage
1 cup sliced carrots
3 cups water
1 (5-ounce) jar Hormel lean dried chipped beef, rinsed and
    shredded
1 (10¾-ounce) can Healthy Request Cream of Mushroom Soup

In a large saucepan sprayed with butter-flavored cooking spray, sauté onion and celery for 6 to 8 minutes or until tender. Add potatoes, cabbage, carrots, and water. Mix well to combine. Bring mixture to a boil. Stir in chipped beef and mushroom soup. Lower heat and simmer for 20 minutes or until vegetables are tender, stirring occasionally.

Each serving equals:

HE: 2½ Vegetable • 1¼ Protein • ½ Bread •
½ Slider • 1 Optional Calorie

172 Calories • 4 gm Fat • 10 gm Protein •
24 gm Carbohydrate • 826 mg Sodium •
100 mg Calcium • 3 gm Fiber

DIABETIC: 1½ Vegetable • 1 Meat • 1 Starch

Frankly Easy Stew ❄

My grandsons love eating anything made with healthy frankfurters, and I suspect most kids do! I love the smoky, tangy flavor of these—served on their own from the microwave or grill, or stirred into a hearty veggie-frank stew like this one.

☻ Serves 4 (1½ cups)

> 8 ounces Healthy Choice 97% fat-free frankfurters, diced
> 1 cup chopped onion
> ½ cup chopped celery
> 1 cup (one 8-ounce can) Hunt's Tomato Sauce
> 2 cups (one 16-ounce can) cut carrots, rinsed and drained
> 1 cup frozen peas, thawed
> 1½ cups (8 ounces) diced cooked potatoes
> 1 teaspoon dried parsley flakes

In a large skillet sprayed with butter-flavored cooking spray, sauté frankfurters, onion, and celery for 8 to 10 minutes or until lightly browned. Stir in tomato sauce, carrots, peas, potatoes, and parsley flakes. Bring mixture to a boil. Lower heat and simmer for 10 minutes or until vegetables are tender, stirring occasionally.

HINT: Thaw peas by placing in a colander and rinsing under hot water for one minute.

Each serving equals:

> HE: 2¾ Vegetable • 1⅓ Protein • 1 Bread
>
> ---
> 177 Calories • 1 gm Fat • 12 gm Protein •
> 30 gm Carbohydrate • 995 mg Sodium •
> 55 mg Calcium • 5 gm Fiber
>
> ---
> DIABETIC: 2 Vegetable • 1 Meat • 1 Starch

Santa Fe Corn and Hot Dog Chowder

Cliff and I are going to be spending more time in the Southwest now that our son Tommy and daughter-in-law Angie have set down roots there, at least for a while. This corn chowder sparkling with bits of tasty frankfurter is "sunny" enough to drive the clouds away, no matter where you live! ☻ Serves 4 (1 cup)

> 1 cup (one 8-ounce can) cream-style corn
> 1 cup frozen whole-kernel corn, thawed
> ½ cup chunky salsa
> 1½ cups (one 12-fluid-ounce can) Carnation Evaporated Skim
>   Milk
> 8 ounces Healthy Choice 97% fat-free frankfurters, diced

In a large saucepan, combine cream-style corn, whole-kernel corn, salsa, and evaporated skim milk. Stir in frankfurters. Cook over medium heat for about 6 to 8 minutes or until mixture is heated through, stirring often.

HINT: Thaw corn by placing corn in a colander and rinsing under hot water for one minute.

Each serving equals:

HE: 1⅓ Protein • 1 Bread • ¾ Skim Milk • ¼ Vegetable

225 Calories • 1 gm Fat • 17 gm Protein • 37 gm Carbohydrate • 979 mg Sodium • 320 mg Calcium • 2 gm Fiber

DIABETIC: 1½ Starch • 1 Meat • 1 Skim Milk

Bean Soups and Chilis

Beans are the stars of many ethnic cuisines, and there's a good reason for it: they're inexpensive, they're satisfying, you can set them to cook for hours and they hold their shape, and best of all, they're full of good nourishment—supplying lots of protein. That's especially helpful if you're preparing meals using less meat than you used to—or even none at all. By serving bean soups and chilis to your family, you can be confident that they're getting the nutrients they need, along with the flavors they love!

We Lunds have always had a special place in our hearts for chili, especially when it's brimming over with meat and beans. My son James has been stirring up his own hot and spicy chili since he was a young boy, and of course Cliff gets downright passionate about just about any Mexican food (he even likes chili on his pizza!). Tommy, on the other hand, turns up his nose at kidney beans, so for him I've created chilis that don't include that "off-limits" legume.

Most of these bean soups and chilis make fantastic main dishes anytime throughout the year, though they're particularly good menu selections during the colder months, where warming the tummy is as important as filling it! I've created recipes featuring many different kinds of beans, from red kidney (sorry, Tommy!) to great northern beans and pinto beans, all of them overflowing with flavor.

If you're in the mood for some blues music, why not stir up some **Memphis Red Beans and Rice Soup** *for a tangy taste of that Southern tradition? For something a little unusual but oh-so-tasty, check out my* **White Chicken Chili**. *And for a dish that will convince your family you've fired up the grill, enjoy the smoky goodness of my* **BBQ Chili**.

Bean Soups and Chilis

Memphis Red Beans and Rice Soup

If there was ever a homemade "cure for the blues," I'd like to think this soup will do the trick! Red beans and rice is as beloved a dining combination as string bass and saxophone is when it comes to playing true Southern blues music. ☻ Serves 4 (1 cup)

1¾ cups (one 14½-ounce can) Swanson Beef Broth
1 (10¾-ounce) can Healthy Request Tomato Soup
1 teaspoon Cajun seasoning
1 teaspoon dried onion flakes
1 teaspoon dried parsley flakes
10 ounces (one 16-ounce can) red kidney beans, rinsed and
    drained
⅔ cup (2 ounces) uncooked Minute Rice

In a large saucepan, combine beef broth, tomato soup, Cajun seasoning, onion flakes, and parsley flakes. Stir in kidney beans. Bring mixture to a boil. Add uncooked rice. Mix well to combine. Lower heat, cover, and simmer for 10 minutes or until rice is tender, stirring occasionally.

Each serving equals:

HE: 1¼ Protein • ½ Bread • ½ Slider •
15 Optional Calories

137 Calories • 1 gm Fat • 6 gm Protein •
26 gm Carbohydrate • 591 mg Sodium •
30 mg Calcium • 5 gm Fiber

DIABETIC: 1½ Starch • 1 Meat

Stormy Weather Bean Soup ❄

Even when there's no sun up in the sky, you'll feel warm and dry as you nourish yourself with this flavorful tummy-pleaser. There's so much protein in a bowl of this soup, whatever the weather, you'll be rarin' to go! ☻   Serves 6 (1½ cups)

> 2 cups water
> 1 full cup (6 ounces) finely diced Dubuque 97% fat-free ham or
>   any extra-lean ham
> ¾ cup chopped onion
> 1 cup shredded carrots
> ½ cup finely chopped celery
> 10 ounces (one 16-ounce can) great northern beans, rinsed and
>   drained
> 10 ounces (one 16-ounce can) pinto beans, rinsed and drained
> 1¾ cups (one 14½-ounce can) stewed tomatoes, undrained
> 2 cups Healthy Request tomato juice or any reduced-sodium
>   tomato juice
> ½ teaspoon dried minced garlic
> 1 teaspoon chili seasoning
> 1 teaspoon dried parsley flakes
> 1 tablespoon lemon juice

In a large saucepan, combine water, ham, onion, carrots, and celery. Bring mixture to a boil. Lower heat and simmer for 15 to 20 minutes or until vegetables are tender, stirring occasionally. Add great northern beans, pinto beans, undrained tomatoes, and tomato juice. Mix well to combine. Stir in garlic, chili seasoning, parsley flakes, and lemon juice. Cover, and continue simmering for 15 to 20 minutes, stirring occasionally.

Each serving equals:

HE: 2⅓ Protein • 2 Vegetable

201 Calories • 1 gm Fat • 14 gm Protein •
34 gm Carbohydrate • 515 mg Sodium •
112 mg Calcium • 9 gm Fiber

DIABETIC: 2 Vegetable • 1½ Meat • 1 Starch

Down Home Bean Pot Soup ❄

Were you the first on your block to purchase a slow cooker, and then the first to put it away when it grew dusty from little use? It's time to bring back that old classic (or pick one up at a yard sale or discount store). How comforting to know you're coming home to find dinner all ready after a long day spent driving the kids more places than you can count! ☻ Serves 6 (1 full cup)

> 2 cups Healthy Request tomato juice or any reduced-sodium tomato juice
>
> 2 cups (one 16-ounce can) tomatoes, chopped and undrained
>
> 1 full cup (6 ounces) diced Dubuque 97% fat-free ham or any extra-lean ham
>
> ½ cup chopped onion
>
> 1 cup shredded carrots
>
> ½ cup chopped celery
>
> 20 ounces (two 16-ounce cans) great northern beans, rinsed and drained
>
> 1½ cups shredded cabbage
>
> 1 teaspoon dried parsley flakes
>
> ¼ teaspoon black pepper

In a slow cooker container, combine tomato juice, undrained tomatoes, ham, onion, carrots, celery, great northern beans, and cabbage. Add parsley flakes and black pepper. Mix well to combine. Cover and cook on HIGH for 30 minutes. Turn setting to LOW and continue cooking for 6 to 8 hours. Stir well before serving.

Each serving equals:

HE: 2½ Vegetable • 2⅓ Protein

189 Calories • 1 gm Fat • 14 gm Protein • 31 gm Carbohydrate • 438 mg Sodium • 112 mg Calcium • 8 gm Fiber

DIABETIC: 2 Vegetable • 2 Meat • 1 Starch

Lazy-Day Bean Soup

No time to cook, or maybe just no inclination today? No matter! This recipe stirs up with ease in about 15 minutes—what could be simpler than that? If you've been looking to increase the amount of fiber in your diet, this soup is a great menu choice.

○ Serves 4 (1 full cup)

½ cup (3 ounces) finely diced Dubuque 97% fat-free ham or any extra-lean ham
20 ounces (two 16-ounce cans) great northern beans, rinsed and drained
1 cup water
1 (10¾-ounce) can Healthy Request Tomato Soup
¼ teaspoon dried minced garlic
2 tablespoons dried vegetable flakes
1 tablespoon dried onion flakes
1 teaspoon dried parsley flakes
2 teaspoons Brown Sugar Twin

In a medium saucepan, combine ham, great northern beans, water, and tomato soup. Stir in garlic, vegetable flakes, onion flakes, parsley flakes, and Brown Sugar Twin. Bring mixture to a boil. Lower heat, cover, and simmer for 10 to 15 minutes, stirring occasionally.

Each serving equals:

HE: 3 Protein • ½ Slider • 6 Optional Calories

242 Calories • 2 gm Fat • 16 gm Protein •
40 gm Carbohydrate • 413 mg Sodium •
108 mg Calcium • 9 gm Fiber

DIABETIC: 2 Starch • 1 Meat

Beans and Franks Chowder

This kid-pleasing favorite will also win the heart of any big kids in your life! Make sure the franks are chopped small so the youngest won't have any trouble swallowing the meaty chunks. This dish is especially protein-rich, so if it appeals to your picky eaters, serve it often to make sure they're getting the nourishment they need.

● Serves 4 (1¼ cups)

10 ounces (one 16-ounce can) pinto beans, rinsed and drained
8 ounces Healthy Choice 97% fat-free frankfurters, chopped
½ cup chopped onion
2 cups (one 16-ounce can) tomatoes, chopped and undrained
1 cup (one 8-ounce can) Hunt's Tomato Sauce
½ cup water
2 tablespoons pourable Sugar Twin
1 teaspoon dried parsley flakes
¼ teaspoon black pepper

In a medium saucepan, combine pinto beans, frankfurters, onion, undrained tomatoes, tomato sauce, and water. Bring mixture to a boil. Stir in Sugar Twin, parsley flakes, and black pepper. Lower heat and simmer for 15 to 20 minutes or until onion is tender, stirring occasionally.

Each serving equals:

HE: 2½ Protein • 2¼ Vegetable • 8 Optional Calories

218 Calories • 2 gm Fat • 15 gm Protein •
35 gm Carbohydrate • 984 mg Sodium •
80 mg Calcium • 8 gm Fiber

DIABETIC: 2½ Vegetable • 2 Meat • 1 Starch

Tuscan Bean and Pastrami Soup

Bean soups are a beloved culinary tradition in Italy, especially in the beautiful hill towns of Tuscany. They're hearty and flavorful, they look as lovely as they taste, and they're perfect for supper with warm bread and a salad. ☻ Serves 4 (1½ cups)

> 10 ounces (one 16-ounce can) great northern beans, rinsed and drained
> 1 cup sliced celery
> 1 (2.5-ounce) package Carl Buddig 90% lean pastrami, shredded
> 1 cup (one 8-ounce can) Hunt's Tomato Sauce
> 1¾ cups (one 15-ounce can) Swanson Beef Broth
> 1¼ cups water
> 1 teaspoon dried minced garlic
> 1 teaspoon Italian seasoning
> 2 cups frozen Italian green beans, thawed
> ¼ cup (¾ ounce) grated Kraft fat-free Parmesan cheese

In a large saucepan, combine great northern beans, celery, pastrami, tomato sauce, beef broth, water, garlic, and Italian seasoning. Bring mixture to a boil. Lower heat, cover, and simmer for 30 minutes, stirring occasionally. Add green beans. Mix well to combine. Continue simmering for 10 to 12 minutes or until green beans are tender, stirring occasionally. When serving, sprinkle 1 tablespoon Parmesan cheese over top of each bowl.

HINT: Thaw green beans by placing in a colander and rinsing under hot water for one minute.

Each serving equals:

HE: 2½ Vegetable • 2 Protein • 16 Optional Calories

154 Calories • 2 gm Fat • 12 gm Protein •
22 gm Carbohydrate • 985 mg Sodium •
79 mg Calcium • 8 gm Fiber

DIABETIC: 2½ Vegetable • 1½ Meat • 1 Starch

Pot Luck Chili

A little of this, a little of that . . . that's one of my favorite ways to create a recipe in a hurry that truly pleases the palate. You'll see that the combo of beans and ground meat delivers a high-protein, high-energy meal-in-a-bowl!   ❂   Serves 8 (1½ cups)

> 20 ounces pinto beans, rinsed and drained ☆
> 16 ounces ground 90% lean turkey or beef
> 2 tablespoons taco seasoning
> 4 cups Healthy Request tomato juice or any reduced-sodium
>   tomato juice
> 1¾ cups (one 15-ounce can) Hunt's Tomato Sauce
> 1 (10¾-ounce) can Healthy Request Tomato Soup
> ½ cup finely chopped onion
> 1 cup chunky salsa
> 1 tablespoon chili seasoning
> 1¾ cups (one 14½-ounce can) Swanson Beef Broth

In a medium bowl, mash half of pinto beans with fork or potato masher. In a large saucepan sprayed with olive oil–flavored cooking spray, combine mashed pinto beans, meat, and taco seasoning. Cook over medium heat until meat is browned, stirring often. Add remaining pinto beans, tomato juice, tomato sauce, tomato soup, onion, salsa, chili seasoning, and beef broth. Mix well to combine. Bring mixture to a boil. Lower heat, cover, and simmer for 30 minutes, stirring occasionally.

Each serving equals:

> HE: 2¾ Protein • 2¼ Vegetable • ¼ Slider •
> 7 Optional Calories
>
> ---
>
> 258 Calories • 6 gm Fat • 18 gm Protein •
> 33 gm Carbohydrate • 853 mg Sodium •
> 95 mg Calcium • 7 gm Fiber
>
> ---
>
> DIABETIC: 2 Meat • 2 Vegetable • 1 Starch

Grandpa's Favorite Chili

I served this to Cliff's dad, Cleland, who's always been a wonderful grandpa to our kids. Like his son, he enjoys things spicy—does that surprise you? I think this contains the perfect amount of chili seasoning, but you can always adjust it to please the favorite grandpa in your life!   ☻   Serves 2 (1¼ cups)

4 ounces ground 90% lean turkey or beef
½ cup chopped onion
½ cup chopped green bell pepper
1 cup (one 8-ounce can) tomatoes, coarsely chopped and
 undrained
1 cup (one 8-ounce can) Hunt's Tomato Sauce
2 teaspoons chili seasoning
6 ounces (one 8-ounce can) red kidney beans, rinsed and drained

In a medium saucepan sprayed with olive oil–flavored cooking spray, brown meat, onion, and green pepper. Add undrained tomatoes, tomato sauce, and chili seasoning. Mix well to combine. Bring mixture to a boil. Stir in kidney beans. Lower heat and simmer for 15 minutes, stirring occasionally.

HINT: Purchase a 16-ounce package of lean ground meat, divide by 4 and freeze 3 portions for future use. Don't forget to date and mark packages.

Each serving equals:

HE: 4 Vegetable • 3 Protein

237 Calories • 5 gm Fat • 17 gm Protein •
31 gm Carbohydrate • 806 mg Sodium •
52 mg Calcium • 9 gm Fiber

DIABETIC: 2 Vegetable • 2 Meat • 1½ Starch

Chili Noodle Soup

Did you know that if you eat beans with rice or noodles, you're already getting what is called a complete protein? That's good news for people eating less meat these days, and it's especially true in this recipe, which provides a good wallop of protein in every serving, but only part of it from meat.   ☻   Serves 4 (1½ cups)

> 8 ounces ground 90% lean turkey or beef
> ½ cup chopped onion
> 1 cup chopped celery
> 2 cups Healthy Request tomato juice or any reduced-sodium
>   tomato juice
> 1 cup (one 8-ounce can) Hunt's Tomato Sauce
> 1¾ cups water
> 2 teaspoons chili seasoning
> 6 ounces (one 8-ounce can) red kidney beans, rinsed and drained
> Scant 1 cup (1½ ounces) uncooked noodles

In a large skillet sprayed with butter-flavored cooking spray, brown meat, onion, and celery. Add tomato juice, tomato sauce, water, and chili seasoning. Mix well to combine. Bring mixture to a boil. Stir in kidney beans and uncooked noodles. Lower heat, cover, and simmer for 20 minutes or until vegetables and noodles are tender, stirring occasionally.

Each serving equals:

HE: 2¾ Vegetable • 2¼ Protein • ½ Bread

---

185 Calories • 5 gm Fat • 15 gm Protein •
20 gm Carbohydrate • 584 mg Sodium •
39 mg Calcium • 6 gm Fiber

DIABETIC: 2½ Vegetable • 2 Meat • 1 Starch

Chili Bean Soup

I always travel with my 8-cup glass measuring bowl (and my whisk) in my carry-on bag, so that no matter where I land—and whether or not my big suitcase makes it there, too—I know I can stir up my Healthy Exchanges recipes with confidence. If you've never owned one of these treasures, treat yourself today—you'll be glad you did, especially when you make this appetizing soup for dinner!

☻ Serves 4 (1 cup)

8 ounces ground 90% lean turkey or beef
¾ cup chopped onion
¼ cup chopped green bell pepper
1 (10¾-ounce) can Healthy Request Tomato Soup

1 cup water
2 teaspoons chili seasoning
1 teaspoon white vinegar
1 teaspoon Brown Sugar Twin
10 ounces (one 16-ounce can) red kidney beans, rinsed and drained

Place meat, onion, and green pepper in a plastic colander and place colander in a glass pie plate. Microwave on HIGH (100% power) for 5 to 6 minutes or until meat is browned, stirring after 3 minutes. In an 8-cup glass measuring bowl, combine browned meat, tomato soup, water, chili seasoning, vinegar, and Brown Sugar Twin. Mix well to combine. Stir in kidney beans. Cover and microwave on HIGH for 6 to 8 minutes, stirring after 3 minutes. Let set for 2 minutes before serving.

Each serving equals:

HE: 2¾ Protein • ½ Vegetable • ½ Slider • 6 Optional Calories

206 Calories • 6 gm Fat • 15 gm Protein • 23 gm Carbohydrate • 286 mg Sodium • 32 mg Calcium • 6 gm Fiber

DIABETIC: 2 Meat • 1 Starch

White Chicken Chili

Are you surprised to discover that not all chilis are red or prepared with beef? The explosion of interest in Southwestern-style cuisine has led to some very imaginative combinations of meat, beans, and sauce, including this one. This dish, a favorite of my son-in-law John, looks especially festive when served in a colorful bowl and garnished with a sprig or two of some home-grown herb.

❍ Serves 4 (1¼ cups)

½ cup chopped onion

1 cup finely chopped celery

2 cups (one 16-ounce can) Healthy Request Chicken Broth

10 ounces (one 16-ounce can) great northern beans, rinsed and drained

1 cup (5 ounces) diced cooked chicken breast

1 cup chunky salsa

1 teaspoon dried parsley flakes

In a medium saucepan sprayed with butter-flavored cooking spray, sauté onion and celery for about 8 to 10 minutes or until tender. Stir in chicken broth, great northern beans, and chicken. Add salsa and parsley flakes. Mix well to combine. Bring mixture to a boil. Lower heat, cover, and simmer for 15 to 20 minutes, stirring occasionally.

HINT: If you don't have leftovers, purchase a chunk of cooked chicken breast from your local deli.

Each serving equals:

HE: 2½ Protein • 1¼ Vegetable • 8 Optional Calories

174 Calories • 2 gm Fat • 19 gm Protein •
20 gm Carbohydrate • 515 mg Sodium •
151 mg Calcium • 5 gm Fiber

DIABETIC: 2 Meat • 1 Vegetable • 1 Starch

Fiesta Chili

I've always believed you can't have too many chili recipes! They're a perfect solution when you've got a crowd to feed, or you're looking for a dish that will survive being reheated and kept warm on a buffet, or even just if you want a fast and filling family meal that doesn't cost a lot to fix. Tune the radio to a station with a Latin beat, and dance a little (it's good exercise!) until dinner's ready. Olé!

● Serves 4 (1¼ cups)

> 8 ounces ground 90% lean turkey or beef
>
> 1 cup chopped green bell pepper
>
> ½ cup chopped onion
>
> ½ cup (one 2.5-ounce jar) sliced mushrooms, drained
>
> 1 cup (one 8-ounce can) Hunt's Tomato Sauce
>
> 2 cups (one 16-ounce can) tomatoes, coarsely chopped and undrained
>
> 2 teaspoons chili seasoning
>
> 10 ounces (one 16-ounce can) red kidney beans, rinsed and drained

In a large saucepan sprayed with olive oil–flavored cooking spray, brown meat, green pepper, and onion. Stir in mushrooms, tomato sauce, undrained tomatoes, and chili seasoning. Add kidney beans. Mix well to combine. Bring mixture to a boil. Lower heat, cover, and simmer for 15 minutes, stirring occasionally.

Each serving equals:

HE: 3 Vegetable • 2¾ Protein

205 Calories • 5 gm Fat • 16 gm Protein •
24 gm Carbohydrate • 517 mg Sodium •
39 mg Calcium • 8 gm Fiber

DIABETIC: 2 Vegetable • 2 Meat • 1 Starch

BBQ Chili

I don't know a man who doesn't love that smoky-rich barbecue flavor, but let's face it, you don't want to drag the grill outside every night. And what about when the weatherman is predicting rain all week long? Here's a way to enjoy that outdoors-over-the-coals taste any time at all. It's speedy, healthy, and hearty, too!

● Serves 4 (1¼ cups)

> 8 ounces ground 90% lean turkey or beef
> ½ cup chopped onion
> ½ cup chopped celery
> 3 cups Healthy Request tomato juice or any reduced-sodium
>   tomato juice
> ¼ cup Heinz Light Harvest Ketchup or any reduced-sodium
>   ketchup
> 2 tablespoons Brown Sugar Twin
> 1 tablespoon chili seasoning
> 10 ounces (one 16-ounce can) red kidney beans, rinsed and
>   drained

In a large saucepan sprayed with butter-flavored cooking spray, brown meat, onion, and celery. Add tomato juice, ketchup, Brown Sugar Twin, and chili seasoning. Mix well to combine. Bring mixture to a boil. Stir in kidney beans. Lower heat, cover, and simmer for 15 minutes, stirring occasionally.

Each serving equals:

HE: 2¾ Protein • 2 Vegetable • 18 Optional Calories

197 Calories • 5 gm Fat • 15 gm Protein •
23 gm Carbohydrate • 202 mg Sodium •
44 mg Calcium • 7 gm Fiber

DIABETIC: 2 Meat • 2 Vegetable • 1 Starch

Aloha Pork Chili

✻

Pork is just about always the main attraction at a Hawaiian luau, but if your muumuu's in the wash and your lei has wilted long ago, you can still relish a culinary *aloha* with this tangy-sweet chili! We eat a lot of lean pork here in Iowa, so I'm always looking for new ways to serve it. Just don't be surprised if your sister-in-law takes one bite and starts to hula around the room!

⊙ Serves 6 (1½ cups)

16 ounces ground 90% lean pork
½ cup chopped onion
1 cup chopped green bell pepper
1 teaspoon dried minced garlic
1¾ cups (one 15-ounce can) Hunt's Tomato Sauce
2½ cups Healthy Request tomato juice or any reduced-sodium
     tomato juice
½ cup water
1 cup (one 8-ounce can) crushed pineapple, packed in fruit juice,
     undrained
2 teaspoons chili seasoning

In a large saucepan sprayed with olive oil–flavored cooking spray, brown pork, onion, green pepper, and garlic. Add tomato sauce, tomato juice, water, undrained pineapple, and chili seasoning. Bring mixture to a boil. Lower heat, cover, and simmer for 20 to 25 minutes, stirring occasionally.

Each serving equals:

HE: 2½ Vegetable • 2 Protein • ⅓ Fruit

171 Calories • 4 gm Fat • 19 gm Protein •
15 gm Carbohydrate • 586 mg Sodium •
38 mg Calcium • 2 gm Fiber

DIABETIC: 2 Vegetable • 2 Meat

Mexicali Frankfurter Chili ❄

We've got so many tasty and healthy protein choices these days, thanks to the hard work of our nation's food producers. I've continued to test all the fat-free and reduced-fat franks as they arrived on the market, just so I could develop recipes that really show them off. This one will satisfy your entire family!

☻ Serves 4 (1½ cups)

1¾ cups (one 15-ounce can) Swanson Beef Broth
⅔ cup (1½ ounces) uncooked elbow macaroni
¼ cup diced onion
1¾ cups (one 14½-ounce can) stewed tomatoes, coarsely chopped and undrained
2 cups Healthy Request tomato juice or any reduced-sodium tomato juice
1 cup frozen whole-kernel corn, thawed
8 ounces Healthy Choice 97% fat-free frankfurters, diced
1 tablespoon chili seasoning
⅛ teaspoon black pepper

In a large saucepan, combine beef broth, uncooked macaroni, and onion. Cook over medium heat for 10 minutes or until macaroni is tender, stirring occasionally. Add undrained tomatoes, tomato juice, corn, frankfurters, chili seasoning, and black pepper. Mix well to combine. Bring mixture to a boil. Lower heat and simmer for 15 to 20 minutes, stirring occasionally.

HINT: Thaw corn by placing in a colander and rinsing under hot water for one minute.

Each serving equals:

HE: 2 Vegetable • 1⅓ Protein • 1 Bread • 9 Optional Calories

230 Calories • 2 gm Fat • 13 gm Protein • 40 gm Carbohydrate • 965 mg Sodium • 79 mg Calcium • 4 gm Fiber

DIABETIC: 2 Vegetable • 2 Meat • 1½ Starch

Dessert Soups

"Soup for dessert?" you may ask doubtfully, uncertain about how a fruity bowlful served warm or cold could be a delicious way to end a meal. You're not alone—many people have never enjoyed a luscious dessert soup or even been aware that sweet soups exist!

Fruit soups are popular in the Scandinavian countries (did you know that Cliff's side of the family originally came from there?). They're also great ways to use up extra fruit, especially those berries that are just this side of extra-ripe. If you're faced with a bumper crop of strawberries this year, or someone brings you a bushel of apples next fall, instead of slicing them up for eating, consider dessert soups a truly refreshing alternative. They can be fruity, creamy, served chilled or pleasantly warm. I think they're an especially attractive choice for a ladies' luncheon or afternoon card party. No matter how you present these inventive recipes (many of which result in pretty pastel colors), your guests will be intrigued and delighted.

*These soups also make lovely appetizers and wonderfully satisfying snacks for you and your family. Some couldn't be simpler in their preparation (**Chilled Raspberry Soup** simply requires a blender and about fifteen minutes). Others provide an abundance of old-fashioned flavor and appearance (**Rhubarb-Strawberry Soup with Dessert Dumplings**). With their intense flavors and attractive colors, dessert soups are simply "the berries!"*

Dessert Soups

Fruit Soup

Dried fruits are wonderfully sweet, but you'll be delightfully surprised to discover that their intense flavor only deepens when you cook them up for a special dessert soup. Some of the guests having lunch in JO's Kitchen Cafe peeked into the kitchen when this was bubbling away on the stove, and they just refused to go home without a taste! ❍ Serves 4 (1 cup)

> 3 cups cold water
> 1 cup unsweetened orange juice
> 1 teaspoon lemon juice
> ¼ cup pourable Sugar Twin
> ½ cup raisins or chopped prunes
> ½ cup (2¼ ounces) chopped dried apricots
> 6 tablespoons Quick Cooking Minute Tapioca
> 1 (4-serving) package JELL-O sugar-free vanilla cook-and-serve
>   pudding mix
> Dash nutmeg

In a large saucepan, combine water, orange juice, lemon juice, Sugar Twin, raisins, apricots, and tapioca. Let set for 10 minutes. Stir in dry pudding mix. Cook over medium heat until mixture just starts to boil, stirring constantly. When serving, lightly sprinkle nutmeg over top of each bowl. Serve warm.

Each serving equals:

HE: 1⅔ Fruit • ½ Slider • 7 Optional Calories

144 Calories • 0 gm Fat • 1 gm Protein •
35 gm Carbohydrate • 82 mg Sodium •
21 mg Calcium • 1 gm Fiber

DIABETIC: 2 Fruit • ½ Starch

Chilled Raspberry Soup

What could be more refreshing and utterly beautiful than this rosy-hued, cool and creamy blend that takes almost no time to prepare! You don't have to wait for a steamy summer afternoon to try this one, but I can promise you that if the mercury is rising and you're feeling hotter than hot, this is a true treat for the taste buds!

✪ Serves 4 (1 cup)

1½ cups frozen unsweetened raspberries
1 cup Ocean Spray reduced-calorie cranberry juice cocktail
1 cup water
½ cup pourable Sugar Twin
¼ teaspoon ground cinnamon
1 cup Yoplait fat- and sugar-free raspberry yogurt
¼ cup Land O Lakes no-fat sour cream

In a blender container, combine frozen raspberries, cranberry juice cocktail, water, Sugar Twin, and cinnamon. Cover and process on BLEND for 10 to 15 seconds. Add raspberry yogurt. Re-cover and continue processing on BLEND for 15 to 20 seconds or until mixture is smooth. Spoon mixture into soup bowls. Refrigerate for at least 15 minutes. When serving, top each bowl with 1 tablespoon sour cream.

Each serving equals:

HE: ¾ Fruit • ¼ Skim Milk • ¼ Slider •
7 Optional Calories

76 Calories • 0 gm Fat • 4 gm Protein •
15 gm Carbohydrate • 72 mg Sodium •
141 mg Calcium • 2 gm Fiber

DIABETIC: 1 Fruit • ½ Carbohydrate

Refreshing Strawberry Dessert Soup

I've got several strawberry patches just outside "The House That Recipes Built," supplying berries for my recipe testing and for use in JO's Kitchen Cafe. But at the height of the season, when those ruby gems are sweet and luscious, I find myself creating strawberry recipes day and night! I've already warned Cliff, I'm going to need a bigger garden! ☻ Serves 4 (1 full cup)

> ¾ cup Diet Mountain Dew ☆
> 4 cups fresh strawberries ☆
> ¾ cup Yoplait plain fat-free yogurt
> ⅓ cup Carnation Nonfat Dry Milk Powder
> Sugar substitute to equal ¼ cup sugar
> ¼ cup Cool Whip Lite

In a blender container, combine ½ cup Diet Mountain Dew and 3 cups strawberries. Cover and process on BLEND for 30 seconds or until mixture is smooth. In a large bowl, combine yogurt and dry milk powder. Stir in sugar substitute. Add remaining ¼ cup Diet Mountain Dew and blended strawberry mixture. Mix well to combine. Finely chop remaining 1 cup strawberries and fold into soup mixture. Refrigerate for at least 30 minutes. When serving, top each bowl with 1 tablespoon Cool Whip Lite.

Each serving equals:

HE: 1 Fruit • ½ Skim Milk • 16 Optional Calories

97 Calories • 1 gm Fat • 5 gm Protein •
17 gm Carbohydrate • 69 mg Sodium •
174 mg Calcium • 2 gm Fiber

DIABETIC: 1 Fruit • ½ Skim Milk

Apple Soup with Raisin Dumplings

Talk about scrumptious! This cozy-warm soup filled the kitchen with such mouth-watering aromas, I began enjoying this dish even before I dipped my spoon into my bowl! It's truly sweet and so satisfying, you'll want to share it with friends and family all winter long! ❍ Serves 4 (1 cup soup and 1 dumpling)

> 1 cup unsweetened apple juice
>
> 2 cups water
>
> 1 (4-serving) package JELL-O sugar-free vanilla cook-and-serve pudding mix
>
> 1½ teaspoons apple pie spice ☆
>
> 1 cup (2 small) cored, peeled, and chopped cooking apples
>
> ¾ cup Bisquick Reduced Fat Baking Mix
>
> 2 tablespoons pourable Sugar Twin
>
> ¼ cup raisins
>
> ⅓ cup skim milk

In a large saucepan, combine apple juice, water, dry pudding mix, and 1 teaspoon apple pie spice. Stir in apples. Cook over medium heat for 6 to 8 minutes or until apples soften, stirring often. Lower heat and simmer. Meanwhile, in a medium bowl, combine baking mix, Sugar Twin, raisins, and remaining ½ teaspoon apple pie spice. Add skim milk. Mix well to combine. Drop batter by tablespoonful into hot mixture to form 4 dumplings. Cover and continue simmering for 10 minutes or until dumplings are firm.

HINT: Great served with ¼ cup sugar- and fat-free vanilla ice cream spooned over top, but don't forget to count the few additional calories.

Each serving equals:

HE: 1½ Fruit • 1 Bread • ¼ Slider •
11 Optional Calories

---

190 Calories • 2 gm Fat • 3 gm Protein •
40 gm Carbohydrate • 390 mg Sodium •
54 mg Calcium • 1 gm Fiber

DIABETIC: 1½ Fruit • 1 Starch

Rhubarb-Strawberry Soup with Dessert Dumplings

This was such a joy to test, we had to make a couple extra batches for all the employees who squeezed into the kitchen pleading for a taste! Rhubarb has always signaled the start of spring for me and provided the first hint that summer is on its way. Well, here's my idea for welcoming those sunny days with enthusiasm!

❍ Serves 4 (¾ cup soup and 1 dumpling)

> 2 cups water
> 1 (4-serving) package JELL-O sugar-free strawberry gelatin
> 3 cups diced fresh or frozen rhubarb
> 1 cup sliced fresh strawberries
> ¾ cup Bisquick Reduced Fat Baking Mix
> 2 tablespoons pourable Sugar Twin
> ⅓ cup skim milk

In a large saucepan, combine water and dry gelatin. Stir in rhubarb. Cover and cook over medium heat for 6 to 8 minutes or until rhubarb softens, stirring occasionally. Add strawberries. Mix well to combine. Lower heat and simmer. Meanwhile, in a medium bowl, combine baking mix, Sugar Twin, and skim milk. Drop batter by tablespoonful into hot mixture to form 4 dumplings. Re-cover and continue simmering for 10 minutes or until dumplings are firm. Serve warm.

Each serving equals:

> HE: 1½ Vegetable • 1 Bread • ¼ Fruit •
> ¼ Slider • 1 Optional Calorie
> _____
> 125 Calories • 1 gm Fat • 5 gm Protein •
> 24 gm Carbohydrate • 330 mg Sodium •
> 127 mg Calcium • 2 gm Fiber
> _____
> DIABETIC: 1 Starch • ½ Fruit

Making Healthy Exchanges Work for You

You're now ready to begin a wonderful journey to better health. In the preceding pages, you've discovered the remarkable variety of good food available to you when you begin eating the Healthy Exchanges way. You've stocked your pantry and learned many of my food preparation "secrets" that will point you on the way to delicious success.

But before I let you go, I'd like to share a few tips that I've learned while traveling toward healthier eating habits. It took me a long time to learn how to eat *smarter*. In fact, I'm still working on it. But I am getting better. For years, I could *inhale* a five-course meal in five minutes flat—and still make room for a second helping of dessert!

Now I follow certain signposts on the road that help me stay on the right path. I hope these ideas will help point you in the right direction as well.

1. **Eat slowly** so your brain has time to catch up with your tummy. Cut and chew each bite slowly. Try putting your fork down between bites. Stop eating as soon as you feel full. Crumple your napkin and throw it on top of your plate so you don't continue to eat when you are no longer hungry.

2. **Smaller plates** may help you feel more satisfied by your food portions *and* limit the amount you can put on the plate.

3. **Watch portion size.** If you are *truly* hungry, you can always add more food to your plate once you've finished your initial serving. But remember to count the additional food accordingly.

4. **Always eat at your dining-room or kitchen table.** You deserve better than nibbling from an open refrigerator or over the sink. Make an attractive place setting, even if you're eating alone. Feed your eyes as well as your stomach. By always eating at a table, you will become much more aware of your true food intake. For some reason, many of us conveniently "forget" the food we swallow while standing over the stove or munching in the car or on the run.

5. **Avoid doing anything else while you are eating.** If you read the paper or watch television while you eat, it's easy to consume too much food without realizing it, because you are concentrating on something else besides what you're eating. Then, when you look down at your plate and see that it's empty, you wonder where all the food went and why you still feel hungry.

Day by day, as you travel the path to good health, it will become easier to make the right choices, to eat *smarter*. But don't ever fool yourself into thinking that you'll be able to put your eating habits on cruise control and forget about them. Making a commitment to eat good healthy food and sticking to it takes some effort. But with all the good-tasting recipes in this Healthy Exchanges cookbook, just think how well you're going to eat—and enjoy it—from now on!

Healthy Lean Bon Appetit!

Index of Recipes

I want to hear from you . . .

Besides my family, the love of my life is creating "common folk" healthy recipes and solving everyday cooking questions in the *Healthy Exchanges Way*. Everyone who uses my recipes is considered part of the Healthy Exchanges Family, so please write to me if you have any questions, comments, or suggestions. I will do my best to answer. With your support, I'll continue to stir up even more recipes and cooking tips for the Family in the years to come.

Write to: JoAnna M. Lund
              c/o Healthy Exchanges, Inc.
              P.O. Box 124
              DeWitt, IA 52742

If you prefer, you can fax me at 1-319-659-2126 or contact me via e-mail by writing to HealthyJo@aol.com. Or visit my Healthy Exchanges Internet web site at http://www.healthyexchanges.com.

Now That You've Seen
Grandma Jo's Soup Kettle, Why Not Order The Healthy Exchanges Food Newsletter?

If you enjoyed the recipes in this cookbook and would like to cook up even more of these "common folk" healthy dishes, you may want to subscribe to *The Healthy Exchanges Food Newsletter*.

This monthly 12-page newsletter contains 30-plus new recipes *every month* in such columns as:

- Reader Exchange
- Reader Requests
- Recipe Makeover
- Micro Corner
- Dinner for Two

- Crock Pot Luck
- Meatless Main Dishes
- Rise & Shine
- Our Small World

- Brown Bagging It
- Snack Attack
- Side Dishes
- Main Dishes
- Desserts

In addition to all the recipes, other regular features include:

- The Editor's Motivational Corner
- Dining Out Question & Answer
- Cooking Question & Answer
- New Product Alert
- Success Profiles of Winners in the Losing Game
- Exercise Advice from a Cardiac Rehab Specialist
- Nutrition Advice from a Registered Dietitian
- Positive Thought for the Month

Just as in this cookbook, all *Healthy Exchanges Food Newsletter* recipes are calculated in three distinct ways: 1) Weight Loss Choices, 2) Calories; Fat, Protein, Carbohydrates, and Fiber in grams; Sodium and Calcium in milligrams; and 3) Diabetic Exchanges.

The cost for a one-year (12-issue) subscription with a special Healthy Exchanges 3-ring binder to store the newsletters in is $28.50, or $22.50 without the binder. To order, simply complete the form and mail to us *or* call our toll-free number and pay with your VISA or MasterCard.

_____ Yes, I want to subscribe to *The Healthy Exchanges Food Newsletter.* $28.50 Yearly Subscription Cost with Storage Binder $_____

$22.50 Yearly Subscription Cost without Binder . . . . $_____

_____ Foreign orders please add $6.00 for money exchange and extra postage . . . . $_____

_____ I'm not sure, so please send me a sample copy at $2.50 . . . . $_____

Please make check payable to HEALTHY EXCHANGES or pay by VISA / MasterCard

CARD NUMBER: _____   EXPIRATION DATE: _____

SIGNATURE: _____
Signature required for all credit card orders.

Or Order Toll-Free, using your credit card, at 1-800-766-8961

NAME: _____

ADDRESS: _____

CITY: _____   STATE: _____   ZIP: _____

TELEPHONE:(   ) _____

If additional orders for the newsletter are to be sent to an address other than the one listed above, please use a separate sheet and attach to this form.

MAIL TO: **HEALTHY EXCHANGES**
P.O. BOX 124
DeWitt, IA 52742-0124

1-800-766-8961 for customer orders
1-319-659-8234 for customer service

Thank you for your order, and for choosing to become a part of the Healthy Exchanges Family!

About the Author

JoAnna M. Lund, a graduate of the University of Western Illinois, worked as a commercial insurance underwriter for eighteen years before starting her own business, Healthy Exchanges, Inc., which publishes cookbooks, a monthly newsletter, motivational booklets, and inspirational audiotapes. Her first book, *Healthy Exchanges Cookbook*, has more than 500,000 copies in print. A popular speaker with hospitals, support groups for heart patients and diabetics, and service and volunteer organizations, she appears regularly on QVC, and on regional television and radio shows, and has been featured in newspapers and magazines across the country.

The recipient of numerous business awards, JoAnna was an Iowa delegate to the national White House Conference on Small Business. She is a member of the International Association of Culinary Professionals, the Society for Nutrition Education, and other professional publishing and marketing associations. She lives with her husband, Clifford, in DeWitt, Iowa.

Healthy Exchanges recipes are a great way to begin—
but if your goal is living healthy for a lifetime,

You need HELP!

JoAnna M. Lund's
Healthy Exchanges Lifetime Plan

"I lost 130 pounds and reclaimed my health following a Four Part
Plan that emphasizes not only Healthy Eating, but also Moderate
Exercize Lifestyle Changes and Goal-setting, and most important of
all, Positive Attitude."

- If you've lost weight before but failed to keep it off . . .
- If you've got diabetes, high blood pressure, high cholesterol, or
  heart disease—and you need to reinvent your lifestyle . . .
- If you want to raise a healthy family and encourage good lifelong
  habits in your kids . . .

HELP is on the way!

- The Support You Need • The Motivation You Want •
  A Program That Works•

HELP: Healthy Exchanges Lifetime Plan is available
at your favorite bookstore.

Other delicious titles by JoAnna Lund available from Putnam:

Dessert Every Night!

ISBN 0-399-14422-6 • $21.95 ($30.00 CAN)

Cooking Healthy
with a Man in Mind
ISBN 0-399-14265-7
$19.95 ($27.99 CAN)

Cooking Healthy
with the Kids in Mind
ISBN 0-399-14358-0 • $19.95 ($26.95 CAN)

HELP: Healthy Exchanges®
Lifetime Plan
ISBN 0-399-14164-2
$21.95 ($30.99 CAN)

Healthy Exchanges® Cookbook
ISBN 0-399-14065-4 • $16.95 ($23.99 CAN)

Available wherever books are sold